Advance Praise for Change

"Kotter's new book, *Change*, is a game changer. He and his co-authors provide deep insight into the misunderstood intersection between logical and psychological business transformation strategies. If you want your business to Survive and Thrive, this book is a must read."

Kelly S. King, Chairman and CEO, Truist Bank

"This is destined to be a wake-up call for a lot of businesses and other enterprises and a classic that will be referred to for a very long time.

"Extremely well written, crisp and to the point, it clearly lays out the concepts and flows seamlessly into the research/examples/cases with a compelling comparison of the 'old way' and the 'new way.' Above all, it articulates the new theories and approaches in very powerful and credible ways."

Bill Deckelman, EVP and General Counsel, DXC Technology Company

"Just as they do in their consulting, the authors of this book make the complex challenge of leading change accessible. It boils down the 'theory of change' into commonsense advice that is actionable and relevant—no matter if you are changing strategy, reconsidering structure, or simply trying to adapt at the speed of today's change. As we prepare for a post-COVID world, never has there been a time when harnessing the imagination and energy of employees has been more critical for companies that want to thrive in an environment that may look completely different than a year ago. This marvelous book can help companies prepare for this massive challenge . . . and opportunity."

Jessica DeVlieger, Global CEO, C Space

"Comprehensive. Integrated. The book helps people like myself look up from short-term pressures and keep a focus on the larger issues we face. It offers a perspective that most CEOs or chairs will immediately understand. And it is hugely relevant to the challenges we face today."

Anthony McCord, Chief Transformation Officer,
New York City Mass Transit Authority

"The background, history, and case studies show a new way of thinking and acting. The lessons are short, to the point, yet profound. This is a call to action for all who care to move from the ranks of management to be key leaders in their companies, industries, and communities."

Douglas Williams, EVP, COO, HMS Holdings

"Different from other books on change, the focus is on three broad sets of critical influencing factors: human behavior hardwiring (to survive and/or thrive), modern organizational structures and how they undercut change, and the notion that leadership can come from everywhere and not just the top. It beautifully captures how almost everyone approaches change today, i.e., top down and metrics driven, as well as a research- and experience-based (vastly better) alternative. The 'dual system' idea is clever and greatly needed because we must have both the reliability, efficiency, and scale afforded by modern organizational structures and the adaptability, agility, and flexibility afforded by fluid networks."

Peter Kim, Vice President, Thermo Fisher Scientific

"Change is everywhere now, yet there is no broadly accepted and effective way to adapt to it. Obstacles slow progress, and the most relevant obstacle to change and innovation is often the very nature of established firms.

"Kotter and his co-authors show in this book how to build a platform able to promote and welcome change. They describe with story after story how to multiply the resources engaged in providing strategic agility, speed, and the like while continuing to deliver ongoing short-term results. They also illuminate how to make your organization ready for the next big set of changes, whatever they are.

"Revealing. Intriguing. Masterful."

Alberto Irace, former CEO of ACEA, Rome Italy

"The Survive/Thrive model is an extremely interesting construct, nicely illustrated throughout the entire book. Between the research and the case studies, the key implications are well covered and the points are clearly made. This makes this book a very practical point of application of brain and behavioral science.

"The first two chapters make an excellent short book just by themselves. Then Chapters 9 and 10 also are extraordinary. The reflection about what social movements can learn from businesses and vice versa is intriguing and thought-provoking. And the proclamation of more leadership from more people makes the reader crave to go look for more ways to democratize leadership."

Antonio Boadas, Chief Communication Officer, Haier/GE Appliances

"Powerful and timely thought leadership that fills a much-needed gap."

Charles Fleet, Chief Transformation Officer, Omnitracs

"This is a great book with a ton of insight, hugely relevant everywhere today. It's even more important in technology, where if you do not change fast enough, you get run over. Think Intel. Self-cannibalization is often key to winning. You cannot 'strategically plan' your way to success in technology.

"Despite the massive pace of events, competition, speed, increased risk, after reading this book you will be left inspired—inspired to press your own change button."

Taner Ozcelik, SVP and Group General Manager, ON Semiconductor

"Change is a science and John Kotter is a master at it. As leaders, we too often act in ways that may have worked in the past but not in our current world of fast-paced change. In *Change*, Kotter, Akhtar, and Gupta explain some of the new science in an easy to understand way, and share their vast experience in what works and what does not when it comes to leading change and getting great business results. If you are already familiar with John Kotter's work, this will be a natural and important continuation of what you've learned. If this is the first time you are reading John Kotter, this can be the book that really makes you thrive at what you do."

Anders Vinther, author and former Chief Quality Officer, Sanofi Pasteur

"In this increasingly complex world, every leader needs this guidebook to enact meaningful change and achieve results. It is another Kotter masterpiece on leadership."

Reihaneh Irani-Famili, Vice President of Business Readiness, National Grid

CHANGE

HOW ORGANIZATIONS ACHIEVE

HARD-TO-IMAGINE RESULTS

IN **UNCERTAIN AND VOLATILE TIMES**

JOHN P. KOTTER

Konosuke Matsushita Professor of Leadership, Emeritus
Harvard Business School
Co-Founder and Executive Chairman, Kotter International

VANESSA AKHTAR

GAURAV GUPTA

Published by John Wiley & Sons, Inc., Hoboken, New Jersey.
Published simultaneously in Canada.

For general information on our other products and services or for technical support, please contact our Customer Care Department within the United States at (800) 762-2974, outside the United States at (317) 572-3993 or fax (317) 572-4002.

Wiley publishes in a variety of print and electronic formats and by print-on-demand. Some material included with standard print versions of this book may not be included in e-books or in print-on-demand. If this book refers to media such as a CD or DVD that is not included in the version you purchased, you may download this material at http://booksupport.wiley.com. For more information about Wiley products, visit www.wiley.com.

Library of Congress Cataloging-in-Publication Data is Available:

ISBN 9781119815846 (Hardcover)
ISBN 9781119815877 (ePDF)
ISBN 9781119815884 (ePub)

Cover Design: Wiley
Cover Image: © pialhovik/Getty Images

SKY1007374_060121

Contents

Preface

By John Kotter

This introductory section is for readers who would like to know more about the evolution of the ideas in this book and the evidence supporting them. If you are not one of those readers, I suggest you consider skipping this section and go directly to Chapter 1.

The roots of the work that led to *Change* began decades ago. At first, I was not focused on change. My interest then, and still today, was on performance, broadly defined. Why do some organizations outperform others? Why do some individual managers and executives produce so much more in terms of valued results? What allows individuals and enterprises to sustain high levels of performance over time? The research itself pulled my attention to the subjects of change and leadership. It provided compelling evidence again and again that the world was moving faster. Coping with the reality of that acceleration was one crucial factor at the core of performance.

Over nearly 50 years, my colleagues at Harvard Business School, and more recently my associates at Kotter International, the consulting firm I helped co-found, have in total launched 16 multiyear research projects. I estimate that we have studied in some depth well over 600 organizations. Most were businesses, but far from all. Research sites also included entities from the health, education, government, religious, and other nonprofit sectors. We have studied countless individual professionals, managers, and executives up close, again mostly but far from entirely in business. Indeed, the very first study in this program was of 20 big-city mayors who were in office during the tumultuous 1960s.

Although the details of how we gathered information varied from project to project, one commonality was an emphasis on getting case-study-like detail using observation and interviews. No project relied entirely on surveys or data sets created by others. The method for making sense of this information might formally be called qualitative pattern analysis. There has been a relentless focus on identifying the sequence of actions that drive successes and failures.

I believe this research program, studying organizational successes and struggles up close in a more rapidly changing world, is the largest of its kind ever undertaken.

In addition, during the last decade, through the Kotter International consulting organization, we have been able to turn research results into accessible playbooks. While working beside people executing those playbooks, we have seen, in detail, how well our expanded understanding of change can make a difference in practical terms. The results: in project after project, we have found executives say something along the lines of the subtitle of this book. In the words of one: "What we have accomplished would have been very hard for most of the staff to ever believe possible two or three years ago."

Reports of our work have been shared through a variety of outlets, including educational programs, *Harvard*

Business Review articles, speeches, blogs, and the main-stream press, but most robustly through books; 21 have been published, and 12 of these have been bestsellers. *Our Iceberg Is Melting* and *A Sense of Urgency* made the *New York Times* list. *Iceberg* was the number-one business book in Germany for a year and in Holland for more than a year.

Lists of the best business or management books of the year have honored 13 of these research reports. *Inc.* magazine, the St. Petersburg Economic Forum, strategy+business, and the Chartered Management Institute, for example, all selected *Accelerate* (2014) as a best-of-year book. *Leading Change* (1996), perhaps the most well known of these reports, has been translated into 26 languages and was chosen by *Time* magazine as one of the 25 most influential management books ever written.

The latest project, which led to this manuscript, formally began four years ago with the formation of a study group at Kotter International that focused on the newest insights from brain science. We quickly concluded that this line of research had developed a great deal in the prior two decades. We decided that there was much convergence in this work with our own observations about "human nature" and its role in resisting or facilitating change and innovation.

Further, it appeared that the combination of insights from brain science, our multidecade research program, a growing list of major consulting experiences, and some pioneering work in business history, organizational studies, leadership, and social anthropology had many important implications for why people struggle with change and what leaders can do to mobilize more successful responses to threats and opportunities. This perspective also gave us new insights into the underlying causal dynamics behind observations we have recorded again and again about why some enterprises outperform others.

And more than ever, this latest round of research has not only strengthened the evidence behind certain propositions but extended previous work in very new and highly actionable ways.

Some of the key themes explored in the pages that follow include:

- A more rapid and complex changing environment, including what is now called disruptive change, may be not just one factor but *the* central force shaping the challenges that organizations and people face nowadays.

- Neither human nature, nor the most common form of the modern organization, are designed to handle anything close to this degree of change. Instead, the strongest built-in emphasis is on stability, efficiency, reliability, quick threat elimination, and most of all short-term survival.

- As a result, there is a growing gap between the rate, amount, and complexity of change outside organizations and the ability of the hardwired enterprise and our human capacity to keep up. This gap presents both a danger and an opportunity as organizations work to agilely adjust, adapt, and get ahead of these contextual realities.

- Nevertheless, at least some enterprises (perhaps many) can be guided to close or reduce this gap. These companies can handle rapid change significantly better than the norm and astonishingly better than those struggling the most. They can be equipped to see relevant external change quickly, invent or adapt responses with speed, and get results that are hard for even their own people to imagine.

- Intentionally and thoughtfully improving individual, team, and organizational ability to respond and accelerate, even just a bit, could have a momentous effect on the lives of many, many millions of people worldwide.

- Over the past few decades, especially in the last four years, we have learned a great deal that has yet to be widely used. Our latest research and advisory-based experiences confirm for the first time that there is a growing science to change, especially large-scale change, which we clearly need to understand and implement as quickly as possible.

Our goal in *Change* is to show, in a concrete and actionable way, how this emerging science—with roots in neuroscience, organizational studies, business history, leadership, and more—can be understood and used to make a much-needed difference.

The list of people who have helped with this work is a long one. It starts with my colleagues at Harvard and extends to my associates and clients at Kotter International. I have been able to include some of these acknowledgments at the end of this book. For now, let me extend to all my deepest thanks.

John Kotter, March 2021

Part I

INTRODUCTION

Chapter 1

Threats and Opportunities in a Rapidly Changing World

A s we write this, we are going through a rather extra-ordinary spike in uncertainty, change, and volatility caused by the COVID-19 pandemic. There is a lot of discussion about what the "new normal" will be in 6 to 18 months. While this conversation is interesting and can be provocative, it is all too often misleading. A focus on this pandemic as a once-in-a-lifetime phenomenon can lead us to be passive and to miss the most important lesson: that this crisis is not an aberration but a spike in a trend that has long and deep roots.

Specifically, the amount, complexity, and volatility of change going on around us has been in general *expanding* in waves since even before the start of the industrial revolution. And virtually all the data says that this trend will continue in any number of ways after the current COVID-19 crisis abates. The potential forces of change are not limited to another pandemic. There are plenty of additional possibilities: artificial intelligence, other disruptive technologies, global integration, as well as social and political movements that now have worldwide impact.

Furthermore, a gap is clearly growing between the amount of change happening around us and the change we are successfully, smartly implementing in most of our organizations and lives. As we will show you in the following chapters, this disconnect is increasingly dangerous, especially when people have been convinced that their continuous incremental improvements are all that is needed.

The risks we are taking are also increasingly unnecessary, because the emerging science of change, outlined in the next chapter, offers steps to mitigate bad outcomes. This information is accessible and actionable. It draws on brain research, business history, organizational studies, leadership, and more. We have found it possible to turn the science into replicable, teachable methodologies and then, in any specific situation, into executable playbooks.

Some enterprises have already tapped into this knowledge base. These companies are mobilizing their people to produce hard-to-imagine results by taking advantage of the opportunities presented by more change. These opportunities also have the potential to add great value to society at large.

"The Storm Is Just Beginning"

On January 16, 2020, Volkswagen Group CEO Herbert Diess told VW's senior managers, "If we continue at our current speed, it is going to be tough.... The storm is just beginning. The era of classic car making is over."

We would only add that both our formal research and our advisory work suggest that the long-term change trend has reached a point where the era of classical business and government may be over or may soon be over.

Whether dealing with threats from low-cost competitors or opportunities for growth from innovative products or acquisitions, organizations today need greater speed and flexibility, sometimes much greater, not just to deal with extraordinary events like COVID-19, but to deal with the shifting reality of our present and future. More broadly, the need to adapt rapidly is equally important for society to resolve threats like climate change or food security, as well as to continue capitalizing on opportunities for progress toward a more equitable and prosperous world.

A few enterprises have become adept at facing these challenges by identifying trends early, changing quickly, and successfully maneuvering at speeds that feel like 100 miles per hour. We will share some of these stories in the pages that follow. We're confident in their integrity because, in most of these cases, we watched these events unfold up close in our advisory work. These leading enterprises are outliers from which you can learn much. And learn we must, because the vast majority of organizations are struggling to adapt at a remotely adequate pace.

The need to adapt is nothing new; after all, Benjamin Franklin said, "When you are finished changing, you are finished." What is new is how often we need to change, the pace at which we need to move, and the complexity and volatility of the context in which we are operating.

The Challenge: A More Volatile, Uncertain, and Rapidly Changing World

For centuries, the world has been speeding up, changing more and more often and in increasingly complicated ways. This trend has accelerated as we've moved from an Industrial Age to an Information Age.

Examples of this increased pace and complexity are easily found. The total number of patents granted by the United States Patent and Trademark Office doubled from 1960 to 1990. Then the number of patents quadrupled in the last three decades. While it took the telephone 75 years to reach 50 million users, cell phones took only 12 years, and the iPhone took just three to hit that milestone. A 2018 IBM study estimated that 90% of all data on the internet was produced in the immediately preceding two years.

The average tenure of companies on the S&P 500 in 1965 was 33 years. Today, it is half that. Reputational risks, though hard to quantify, have certainly increased with the growing use of social media, constant news alerts, and venues for publicly accessible employee feedback. Glassdoor has 32 million unique visitors each month. These examples are representative of changes that can be found in many different contexts.

The increased change around us drives an increased effort to change within the organizations that employ us, supply us with needed goods and services, and govern us. There are many variations of what this looks like by industry, sector, or region. But in general, the sheer number of organizational initiatives to produce change is now much larger than 30 years ago. Fifty years ago, virtually no organizations talked about changing their cultures, while today this is commonplace. The growing number of initiatives has led to more and more companies adopting formal project management offices (PMOs).

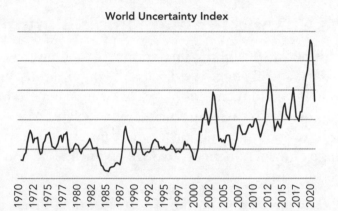

World Uncertainty Index

Source: Adapted from Ahir H, N Bloom, and H Furceri (2018) "World Uncertainty Index", Stanford mimeo. The WUI is computed by counting the percent of the word "uncertain" (or its variants) in the Economist Intelligence Unit country reports.

Along with, and directly related to, the increase in the pace and complexity of change, the last two decades have seen a steep increase in the level of uncertainty. Complex change does that. The high level of economic and political uncertainty can make it difficult to know what initiatives will be necessary to stay competitive and to take advantage of new opportunities.

Unfortunately, as we will see in the examples laid out in this book, the internal change in organizations is not keeping pace with external change and volatility. This challenge affects *everything:* the quality and availability of health care; the stock market; the environment; the affordability of products that make life easier, more interesting, or more fun; the economy; the responsiveness of government; poverty; our ability to deal with medical emergencies, including pandemics; how many of us will lead comfortable and satisfying lives; even how many of us will die needlessly. The list is endless.

The Change Problem and Solution

In this book, we will dig into this increasing uncertainty, volatility, and change. We discuss the implications, as we now understand them, for people who are trying to make things better for their enterprises (and society). We argue that if we continue to improve our capacity to adapt and change only incrementally, we are taking a huge and unnecessary risk.

The good news is that we have learned much over the past few decades about why so many people and organizations struggle with change, why a minority thrive, and why more than a few literally do not survive. As you will see, for perfectly understandable but correctable reasons, much of this knowledge is not yet used in most organizations.

Our collective struggle with change often seems to be the result of ill-equipped, seemingly incompetent, or stubbornly myopic people. The stories of companies like Kodak, Blockbuster, or Borders are often told as cases of arrogant, stubborn leaders who refuse to see what should have been obvious. In hindsight, we question whether they even tried to change. To some degree these critiques are true. But they are not the whole story and hence are misleading.

The bigger story is that neither the core of human nature, hardwired into us many thousands of years ago, nor the central design of modern organizations, very much a late nineteenth- and early twentieth-century invention, were built to change quickly, easily, and smartly. People and organizations were designed mostly to be efficient and reliable enough to ensure survival. We do have the capacity to innovate and create new habits or products. But that capacity is not the most powerful force except in young people and organizations. With maturity comes all sorts of mechanisms that lean toward stability and short-term safety. So even when companies recognize new threats, they are often unable to change enough or fast enough to overcome these challenges.

THE CHANGE PROBLEM (AND OPPORTUNITY)

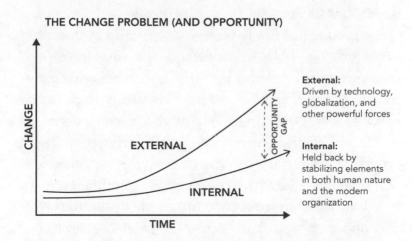

Today, in a more complex and rapidly evolving twenty-first century, when we put a person designed for a world long gone into an organization that was not designed for this century, we regularly see too slow a pace of change in the face of uncertainty. We see too painful a process as individuals and organizations try to deal with inevitable transformation challenges. We get too little too slowly in terms of needed results, even though that deficit is not always obvious.

This struggle is today's reality and potentially tomorrow's catastrophe. *But it does not have to be that way*. Much more is possible.

We know this is true because we have seen examples of success where the gap between external and internal change is minimized or eliminated. When this correction is made, enterprises can leap into new and better futures with widely shared benefits.

Outstanding success is often attributed to a few larger-than-life leaders. There is truth in the observation that an individual can have an outsized impact in certain situations. But both research and our advisory experiences pretty clearly show that the most successful change comes from mobilizing more leadership from many more people. And three streams of research, discussed in the next chapter, seem to be particularly promising in providing insights into how to unleash this expanded idea of leadership. The first stream comes from brain science and deals with human nature and our response to threats and opportunities. The second is from organizational studies and business history and speaks to the limitations of the modern "management-centric" organization and how we can overcome those limitations. The third comes from a branch of leadership studies, one that specifically deals with the all-too-common pitfalls of leading change.

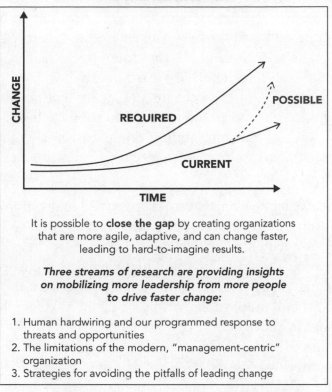

THE CHANGE SOLUTION

It is possible to **close the gap** by creating organizations that are more agile, adaptive, and can change faster, leading to hard-to-imagine results.

Three streams of research are providing insights on mobilizing more leadership from more people to drive faster change:

1. Human hardwiring and our programmed response to threats and opportunities
2. The limitations of the modern, "management-centric" organization
3. Strategies for avoiding the pitfalls of leading change

Taken together, these research streams can provide powerful insights into how you can realistically mobilize much more leadership from many more people to drive change faster and smarter and, thus, to close the gap between internal and external realities.

What is perhaps most encouraging is that we can say, with confidence, that this emerging science of change has gone beyond academic analysis to actual, often dramatic, impact in the real world. Throughout this book, we share examples where organizations have taken a substantially different path from the norm by utilizing methods and insights from this emerging science. What is equally as encouraging is that there is no magical sauce or impossible-to-replicate situation in these examples. We have seen, up close, again and again, that people can be guided, facilitated, educated, and motivated to adopt new ways of thinking and working, to actually change their actions, resulting in sometimes astonishing business or mission impact.

The companies that we discuss (and many more that we do not) have truly done some amazing things. They have implemented whole new strategies to help them roar out of financial crises. They have accomplished, in 90 days, changes and business results that were thought to be totally impossible within a year or two, much less in such a short period of time. These enterprises have significantly improved employee engagement and have seen their efforts reflected in winning awards for Best Place to Work. Big, older companies that have struggled to innovate have developed remarkably successful innovations in products, ways of working, and strategies. Some have changed smartly and swiftly and doubled or tripled their share prices in 2–3 years, or even less.

When you start to add up the people touched with such efforts, the numbers grow big quickly. These improvements are at the heart of Kotter International's vision of "millions leading, billions benefiting." Real results like these are the product not just of research, but useable research. This is why we have organized the book in ways that make it immediately applicable to specific changes you might be experiencing or contemplating.

The Stakes

In a world where billions of people continue to lead lives few of us would want to conceive of, where we face growing environmental challenges that threaten to impact our children and grandchildren disastrously, where emerging technologies in the wrong hands or used for the wrong purposes could be horrific, where biological agents can spread with terrifying speed, and where even in rich countries inequity and inequality raise serious questions about the viability of democracies, *we need (and can create) a lot more change that astounds*.

Experiences that have left people disappointed, pessimistic, or cynical will raise questions about that assertion. But there is sufficient evidence in the research, especially the success stories, to support optimism.

This evidence comes from cases where bold new strategies are not partially but wholly executed within accelerated time frames; where digital transformations do not disrupt business, cost a fortune, and take forever; where restructurings create great efficiencies without killing productivity, morale, or innovation; where remarkably fast and smooth M&A integration eliminates clashing mindsets and all the problems that creates; and perhaps most difficult of all, where real substantial cultural change propels firms into a much better future.

There is a line of thought, typically traced back to the great economist Joseph Schumpeter, that suggests that the problem of change has a better solution than the one we offer here. Schumpeter's solution is called "creative destruction." For example, if government would stop protecting bigger and older enterprises and instead make it easier for entrepreneurs, the dinosaurs who can't adapt would die off and be replaced by innovative youngsters. We would not need to teach the slow-moving or out-of-touch companies to be agile. Instead, we would just let them go extinct when they can no longer keep up.

Of course, creative destruction does happen in our world today, just not in the pure form that some would advocate. The pure form is unrealistic because capital and product markets would struggle to adapt to this constant birth-death dynamic. And labor markets would do more than struggle. They would fail in their attempts to swiftly move massive numbers of unemployed into very different jobs, demanding very different skills, usually in very different parts of the country or the world. Unemployment above a certain point would not only create massive pain to individuals and families, but would undermine faith in capitalism and democracy—perhaps faith in any form of government or economic system.

The clock is ticking. The gap between what is needed and what most organizations are capable of continues to widen. Bringing an organization up from poor performance to the norm is useful and will potentially benefit many people. But going from an F or D grade to a B is not what the world needs. Good is no longer good enough. Even for large numbers of organizations, good still means wasted resources, results coming too slowly, wealth left unrealized, and ultimately people suffering. Rising up from the norm to enter the top 10%, but doing so over 20 years, is no answer, either. Too much is moving too fast for thinking in terms of two decades.

When it came to change, risk mitigation traditionally meant a bias toward caution. Increasingly, risk mitigation means getting on with it and not missing opportunities. In today's world, not adapting fast enough is the greatest risk. Yes, be deliberate and use results from the latest research as a guide. Employ insights from truly outstanding success stories. Learn from people who have been involved in those stories. *But get after it.*

Our goal in this book is to inspire you to embrace change and "get after it!"

And why not? The vast majority of the time, people who successfully help us deal better with change benefit greatly themselves. They not only do better in their careers but they feel better about life. They not only receive material rewards; they gain esteem. They not only survive; they truly thrive. And they leave legacies of which they are deeply proud.

The challenges that businesses—and even more broadly, humanity—face are not small. As the coronavirus pandemic demonstrated, it is no understatement to say that our ability to adapt and respond to these challenges is not only a question of creating prosperity but indeed one of survival.

So much more is needed—and, with a better understanding of some core components of human nature, of the limitations of the design of modern organizations, and of the leadership needed and possible in this era—as you will shortly see, so much more is possible.

Chapter 2

The Emerging Science of Change

The number of different beliefs about why people and organizations often struggle with more change is far from small. The same can be said about the number of possible solutions for how you might mobilize individuals or enterprises to adapt more swiftly and intelligently. The great number of possibilities can leave one confused or even with a sense that few useful generalizations can be made in this soft and convoluted realm.

In fact, we have reached a point where our very understanding of change is changing. There is today what might best be called an emerging science of change—especially the complex, transformational change that needs to happen more often, at faster speeds, and even under conditions of greater uncertainty. This new science tells us much about why people struggle with change, why a few succeed, what the latter do differently, and how we can use this knowledge in our own organizations.

As introduced in Chapter 1, this emerging science—with a set of concepts and principles and tactics—has three major root systems. One system involves the study of individuals: specifically, our "human nature" and resistance to or capacity for change. This study is based on research that goes back centuries but has recently been enhanced greatly with a trove of new material from brain science.

A second root involves the study of the modern organization, work that seriously took off in the 1930s and 1940s. Peter Drucker's *The Concept of the Corporation* was the most visible early example. Some very informative projects in this tradition have come in the past decade.

The third area is the actual study of modern organizations and the people in them trying to lead change, with commentary on outcomes and speculation about causality. Initial examples of this work can be found in the 1950s, but most of this information is much more recent. This increased work on internal change and leadership very much parallels the increase in the rate of contextual change around organizations.

Human Hardwiring: The Survive/Thrive System

Although we have talked about human nature for centuries, only recently have we been able to combine intense observational research with methods that are able to map the hardwiring of the brain and body. The implications of this research stream can be huge, as we will demonstrate in our discussion of strategy, digital transformation, restructuring, cultural change, M&A, scaled Agile, and broad social initiatives.

With our focus on prospering in a more rapidly changing and complex world, the most useful picture that emerges from this research is not the way that most people think about human nature. *In particular, the vast majority of people tend to seriously underestimate the power of our built-in survival instinct and how it can inadvertently overwhelm our capacity to swiftly see opportunities, innovate, adapt, lead, and change for the better.*

Humans have within them something we call the Survive Channel. It has the biological equivalent of a radar system that is constantly on the lookout for threats. At first, a very long time ago, these were probably mostly physical threats. Today, the same basic hardware is programmed by society and personal experiences to be alert to career, economic, psychological, and other perceived hazards to our well-being.

When our brain detects what is perceived to be a danger, a lightning-quick, subconscious sequence of actions occurs. First, our amygdala instantly sends a signal to our brain's "control center" (the hypothalamus). This signal activates the mechanism (our sympathetic nervous system) that is responsible for responding to potentially dangerous situations. Epinephrine (better known as adrenaline) flows through our bodies, increasing heart rate and blood pressure, accelerating breathing to increase oxygen to the blood stream, and releasing blood sugar and fats to prepare us to confront or escape the problem ("fight or flight"). When this happens, our minds tend to focus like a laser on the perceived threat. We use our spiked energy and total focus to try to move quickly to eliminate the hazard. When we are successful, the perceived problem is resolved, the chemicals stop flowing, we calm down, and the body resets to where it was before the "attack."

We have all experienced this Survive response working well countless times in our personal and professional lives. Sometimes it happens much like it did with our ancestors. We start to step off a curb to cross the street when, through our peripheral vision, our Survive radar sees a bus racing our way. Instantaneously, chemicals are released, blood rushes to muscles, all other thought stops, and we jump back onto the sidewalk. This series of events happens in one or two seconds, often before we realize what we've done.

More frequently today, Survive is dealing with more nuanced complexity, and reflects the needs and requirements of life in the more complicated reality of the twenty-first century. A colleague alerts us that one of our biggest customers is irate because of a missing shipment. Our radar reports a threat alert, chemicals flow, our heartbeat increases, our minds forget about other issues as we immediately go to a conference call, virtual meeting, or into a conference room. Six of us gather to review what we know about the problem and plot our options for remedying the missed shipment and helping the unhappy client. Each of us accepts some area of responsibility, completes our tasks, and, after a tense 24 hours, we are told the problem has been solved. The customer seems to be impressed by our fast attention to the issue.

The Survive Channel is a *very* powerful part of our nature. It is certainly central to the fact that humanity has not been wiped out over the last hundred thousand years, unlike millions of other species. But when our brains evolved a long time ago, the world was very different. While this channel is still critical to our survival by allowing us to deal with real threats when they do arise, under the vastly different conditions we now face, our Survive Channel does not always serve us well.

Today, when we are not successful at eliminating some problem, typically because the threats are hugely complex and there is no practical way to avoid or stop them quickly, we can end up in a heightened survival state for a considerable period of time. Our bodies release additional chemicals (cortisol and other hormones), which keep us on high alert. But this intensity drains energy and makes us feel increasingly stressed. Even worse, if we are hit by multiple threats at once, or threats we cannot resolve, we can go into an overheated Survive state. In this condition, we become so tired and distracted that we are unable to deal well with even the problems for which the Survive Channel was designed. We might end up basically running in circles, withdrawing, or freezing. All this tends to overwhelm our capacity to see opportunities, to step back and creatively contemplate, much less to actually change our behavior to quickly capitalize on any opportunities. And how can we rally others to seize opportunity when we can barely function ourselves?

In today's rapidly changing world, with more threats and opportunities, it is not at all unusual for people to have an overheated Survive response, either because of the sheer volume of perceived threats or because we live in an environment with all sorts of barriers that stop us from eliminating even single threats.

Examples of companies in a state of overwhelmed Survive are easily found. A few years ago, a well-known consumer products business had overcapacity relative to demand. They had too much capacity in the wrong geographic and product areas, and a low-cost competitor who had successfully used new technology to reduce expenses and take market share. The executive committee of the challenged firm did what they had all seen done before: they launched a restructuring. When word got out that layoffs were coming, not just individuals but whole parts of the enterprise began moving into overheated Survive. Anxiety (and anger and stress) went up. Morale went down. Productivity slipped. Innovation was overwhelmed by all this Survive exhaustion, along with its narrowly threat-focused minds.

None of these issues stopped the executive committee from doing what it reluctantly had concluded was needed to restore competitiveness. Costs were cut, a few facilities were shut down, and people were laid off. It was not draconian, but it was unpleasant for all involved.

Two years later, the restructuring was officially "complete" and was by some standards a success. Costs had been significantly cut where demand was not needed. But productivity slips dampened the savings.

More importantly, little to no product innovation had occurred during the entire restructuring effort, despite the fact that there were programs in place to create new offerings. Three decades earlier, this pause in effective new product development would have mattered little in a slower-moving world. But this time, two younger competitors swiftly addressed market changes with successful new offerings, gained market share, and in the process created new supply-demand imbalances for the restructured firm.

The CEO took an early retirement. His replacement launched a number of new cost-cutting initiatives and tried to push hard from the top on the product development process. But none of this created the magnitude of needed results. A flawed understanding of what created the firm's problems inevitably led to flawed solutions for fixing them. It always does.

And there *are* solutions. But to find them you need to understand both the Survive Channel and its newer, less dominant companion, the Thrive Channel.

The Thrive Channel also has a radar system, but instead of looking for threats, it seeks opportunities. When Thrive spots possibilities, an internal mechanism is activated (the parasympathetic nervous system) that sends out a different set of chemicals than Survive (like oxytocin and vasopressin). In the Thrive response, our energy goes up but does not spike. Thrive is accompanied by emotions like passion and excitement rather than anxiety or anger. Our field of focus does not shrink; it often does the opposite, expanding as curiosity about the opportunity broadens one's field of vision. When a response is not activated to worry about our own immediate and personal survival, and with positive emotions flowing instead, we are more open to collaboration, creativity, and innovation. The mind and body search for ways to move toward the opportunity. As long as we see evidence that we are making some progress, our increased energy can be sustained for a remarkably long period of time without feeling burned out.

WHEN HARDWIRING WORKS WELL

SURVIVE	THRIVE
THREAT-SEEKING RADAR	OPPORTUNITY-SEEKING RADAR
(Chemicals release)	(Chemicals release)

BRAIN + BODY + EMOTIONS	BRAIN + BODY + EMOTIONS
Laser-focused	Perspective broadens
Energy spikes	Energy increases
Fear, anxiety	Passion, excitement

BEHAVIOR	BEHAVIOR
Fast problem-solving	Innovation, collaboration

A basic reality today is that the way to create enough smart change at a fast enough speed is both to prevent the Survive Channel from overheating and to activate the Thrive Channel across a sufficient number of people. For many reasons, organizations struggle with this challenge.

Companies struggle most fundamentally because a variety of changes in the past few decades have in general overstimulated Survive. This problem stretches from the C-suite to the front line and it easily blocks sufficient

Thrive activation. The more widespread availability and use of data, for example, has in many ways been a boon to producing reliable results, occasionally even helping to spot new opportunities. But the constant barrage of data and metrics, each potentially indicating a problem, can also easily overstimulate Survive. We will have more to say about this later in the book.

The increasingly 24/7 connected world can also add to constant Survive triggering. The 4 a.m. email can be understood by our brains as a crisis, even when it is not. The same is possible for the text message that unexpectedly disturbs our morning coffee.

Social media, with its infinite capacity to make us compare ourselves unfavorably to others, can be a Survive activator. And social media has been touching more and more of our lives, as a source of both benefits and unintended problems.

Our Survive radar has been put on high alert by the personal and professional threats caused by COVID-19. Threats that can cause prolonged uncertainty about our health, the health of those we love, the nature of work, and the global economy seem to come at us on the nightly news with increasing frequency.

The greater availability of global information also gives us much more to worry about. Terror attacks far away, along with natural disasters on other continents, may not be rational threats to us now, but the Survive Channel is not a rational mechanism.

And we have little control, if any, over so many of the "threats" our Survive Channel sees. All of these factors taken together are a perfect recipe for an overheated Survive.

Enough of us have seen the problems caused by an overactivated Survive that we sometimes think we need to move out of a Survive mode. People have often said to us, "We are moving from Survive to Thrive!" and, implicitly, "Isn't that great?" But, in fact, a *well-functioning* Survive greatly aides Thrive activation. Neither underactivated nor overheated, and with a repertoire of effective responses to the problems at hand, a well-functioning Survive Channel is neither a debilitating distraction nor a lethal energy drain. Then, without the need for a Herculean effort, Thrive can be activated through the visibility of inspiring opportunities and the willingness, support, and ability to pursue those opportunities.

We have learned much about how all this happens, not the least through the literature on great leaders throughout history. The best leaders keep Survive alert but not overwhelmed. They also tend to be very good at activating Thrive in themselves and in others. In the past few decades, we have also learned much about how organizations without larger-than-life leaders can still effectively lead major change—where "lead" (not just "manage") is the key word. We will discuss these findings and report stories that demonstrate what is possible throughout this book.

The "Modern" Organization

The second stream of research that informs our emerging theory of change focuses on the modern organization. We say "modern" because it is a relatively new phenomenon.

In the U.S. and most of the more economically developed world, organizational designs that we often assume have been around for millennia, if only in governments and armies, were really not created until the latter decades of the nineteenth century.

The modern organization draws upon practices and lessons from many hundreds of years of human experience but is nevertheless fundamentally different from what came before it. New technologies that began to evolve from the Industrial Revolution allowed for much less expensive production and distribution and created mass markets like never seen before. But capitalizing on these new possibilities required a scale and complexity of organization that had only begun to emerge in a few limited contexts (like textiles and railroads). This new form could accommodate not just the traditional two to ten individuals located at one site but could coordinate thousands of people disbursed geographically in ways unseen before.

To make this complex coordination work and not devolve into chaos, all sorts of new and formal systems, policies, structures, and jobs were invented. Planning was designed as a much more structured process attached to financial budgeting. Reporting relationships and jobs were written into published hierarchical organizational structures. Financial and other control systems were invented to monitor activity everywhere and to make sure results were on plan. New problem-solving techniques and communication methods emerged to make course corrections if results slipped off plan.

And a whole new set of jobs—what today we would call middle management—was created to make these more complex organizations function as they were designed. "Managers" drove "managerial processes," which produced unprecedented efficiencies and a level of reliability that was once thought impossible with large and/or dispersed groups of people.

These new organizations were capable of change. But the default setting was filled with rules, policies, procedures, plans, and a drive toward standardization—all essential for efficiency and reliability, but all potential barriers to change. As long as the world swirled at an acceptably slower-than-today pace, all was mostly okay. Businesses and ever bigger governments struggled to adapt quickly because of the organizational barriers and because of human nature. But "quickly" by today's standards was rarely an issue—until recently.

In the past century and a half, this new form of organization has come to rule the landscape. In some contexts, it has evolved to become much more change-sophisticated. It does so with now commonly used ideas like interdepartmental task forces, less "bureaucracy," and more cultural tolerance for new ideas. But even more so, today's organizations use new, or new versions of, strategy, digital transformation, restructuring, cultural change, M&A, Agile (the software development methodology), and more to help them adapt or capitalize on opportunities created by external changes.

These methodologies can help hugely in this new era of turbulence and uncertainty. But more often than not, even in high-tech settings where people think they have evolved way past Industrial Age organizations, our research shows the typical approaches are currently working only up to a point. Beyond that point, bodies designed for lifelong, long gone and organizations designed fundamentally for a slower-moving and more predictable world both struggle—or at least miss the big opportunities. Smart people see the need to change, and quickly. But far too often they fail to achieve their aspirations. And a feeling that you can only move at 30 or 60 miles an hour, in a context where excelling requires 100 or even 200, can be exceptionally frustrating and stressful.

But it does not have to be this way. Step 1 in changing organizations for the better is recognizing the limitations of the modern form and where those came from. Step 2 is to look at how organizations can realistically be modified to handle both the tasks of reliability and efficiency and the tasks of speed and agility, which we will discuss and demonstrate with stories throughout the book.

Leading Change: Success and Failure

The third stream of research contributing to our emerging theory of change has explicitly focused on observing organizations and individuals in them as they try to purposefully adapt to a shifting context. It also draws on both historical and contemporary studies of leadership.

In an early, foundational piece of this research, we found that transformation efforts failed when there was an insufficient sense of urgency to deal with a faster-moving world. Problems were exacerbated when too small a group, lacking broadly relevant knowledge, connections throughout the organization, leadership skills, and/or a strong sense of urgency was put in charge of driving complex change. This often led to an underdeveloped and undercommunicated strategic vision.

Without sufficient communication of a rational and emotionally compelling case for change, it was nearly impossible to achieve buy-in that inspired and mobilized the action required to drive and sustain difficult changes. Management was resistant to ceding control and too often got in the way of broad-based action. Short-term wins were insufficient to provide credibility and momentum, and when they did occur, they were not celebrated early enough or often enough, which caused any built-up urgency to falter.

When successes were seen, there was a tendency to declare victory too soon and stop short of the finish line. People also underestimated how fragile new changes were, and didn't take the time to truly institutionalize them in the organization's systems and structures.

Our understanding of successful change (and common pitfalls) has continued to deepen and expand based on a number of follow-up studies that continue to add detail and nuance. These studies have addressed the more recent consequences of an increasingly complex, uncertain, and fast-moving world.

In addition to reinforcing the original failure points outlined above, we have seen that the most successful large-scale change efforts start with a clearly articulated, compelling, and emotionally inspiring opportunity. In an increasingly complex world, with more threats and potential problems being thrown at us every day, it is becoming harder and harder to mobilize sustained action through a "burning platform." The burning platform approach creates anxiety, anger, guilt, and stress, which can crush complacency but can too quickly wear us out or result in a sort of frozen, deer-in-the-headlights, Survive Channel panic.

Studies of larger-than-life leaders (Lincoln, Matsushita, Mandela) give us many clues as to how change can be handled well today. The very best of these people created a broadly embraced sense of urgency around opportunity. They communicated widely and got people to buy into the concept of capitalizing on that opportunity. They won over hearts and minds with strategy and passion. They mobilized many to take aligned action against the various organizational and human barriers through relentless positive energy and talk of opportunity. They made sure wins came early and often and were broadcast and celebrated, helping refuel excitement. They were also sensitive to maintaining urgency and energy until work on initiatives was successfully completed.

It is now increasingly clear that these larger-than-life leaders avoided common pitfalls and mobilized action not just intermittently, not just once, but all the time, iteratively, often for years. Our most recent research is showing that's precisely what organizations need to do in a new era of speed, complexity, and uncertainty—similar actions taken not once a decade but continuously.

The net result of all this activity often astounds people. As a result, they may come to see these leaders as highly compelling, heroic, or charismatic. However, the causality often runs in a different direction. It is less that *charisma* mobilizes others to produce astounding results and more that Thrive-activating *behavior* (grounded in an understanding of human nature, modern organizations, and leading change) mobilizes people to produce outstanding results despite all the barriers. This accomplishment creates a perception that the "leader" is heroic and charismatic.

This last point is important because it helps explain why organizations without larger-than-life leaders—which is to say, almost all entities—can also produce astonishing results. They can use diverse teams that create a very similar process of mobilizing and leading others to achieve great change.

Research on leading change successfully today shows that teams drive broad-based action by behaving according to a set of guiding principles.

First, they hold themselves and others accountable to have-to tasks, but they also realize that a want-to, emotionally positive, almost volunteer attitude is essential in mobilizing people to go on a rapid-change journey. Second, they are rational and analytical, but they also win over hearts to get true buy-in, energized volunteerism, and that want-to positive attitude. Third, they are good at management and they develop and promote excellence in the planning, organizing, and controlling so central to modern organizations. But much more than is common today, they also encourage and support leadership from many people, not just from a few of their peers at the top of an organization. Fourth, they use small, highly select groups to attack certain change tasks. Yet they also heavily rely on the diverse many—a group big enough and with the breadth of information and contacts both to figure out what changes are needed and to execute them despite human nature and organizational barriers.

Together, these four points can be thought of as guiding principles associated with accelerating change in complex organizations. They help drive a momentum-building process of leadership that inspires buy-in and action, which creates more leadership, which overcomes more organizational and human barriers, which gets results, which creates more and more opportunity.

CHANGE PRINCIPLES

HAVE TO + WANT TO

Those who feel included in a compelling opportunity will help create change in addition to their normal responsibilities. Creating an emotionally positive experience will help mobilize meaningful action.

HEAD + HEART

Building buy-in based purely on a rational and analytical business case is challenging. If you can engage people's emotions and give greater meaning to your effort, extraordinary results are possible.

MANAGEMENT + LEADERSHIP

In order to capitalize on windows of opportunity, leadership must be paramount—and not just from one executive. It's about vision, action, innovation, and celebration, as well as essential managerial processes.

SELECT FEW + DIVERSE MANY

More people need to be able to make change happen—not just carry out someone else's objectives. Done right, this uncovers leaders at all levels of an organization, unleashing the power of the masses.

Because a management hierarchy can fight this process and is not designed to foster volunteerism, a want-to attitude, and leadership up and down the hierarchy, the most successful change teams now create a second system to facilitate the work, a system built not on formal hierarchy but on fluid networks.

That is, though modern enterprises are organized for good reasons by hierarchy, especially to create efficiency and reliability, change leadership teams also use fluid networks of people to tackle most of the big-change tasks. They create what we have called a "dual system." Hierarchy and controls are central mechanisms to executing operating plans. Networks and leadership from the diverse many are at the core of driving strategic initiatives. This dual system is critical in reinforcing, sustaining, and embedding business outcomes and new ways of working associated with a successful change effort. We will have more to say about this later.

The Three Streams

Taken together, these three streams of research show us why we struggle with change, why the struggle will only grow unless we act now, and what highly effective action increasingly means.

Furthermore, these same principles and processes appear to apply to all complex change challenges and change methodologies, whether they are seen as and labeled as digital/IT, cultural, or even cost cutting (restructuring).

This insight is not widely recognized. Mergers and acquisitions, for example, are treated as a totally different set of tasks than digital transformation. Restructuring is treated as a whole different activity than employing Agile principles. Yet these, as well as some other arenas, all share a very basic reality. They are methods used to help organizations accelerate adaptation or transformation to try to take advantage of a more rapidly changing and volatile world.

More often than not, as you will see in the upcoming chapters, people succeed or struggle in all these areas for the very same reasons—reasons that are less related to digital technologies or M&A genius or Agile or restructuring, and more to do with change principles and processes, the nature of modern organizations, and human Survive and Thrive hardwiring.

THERE'S A SCIENCE TO CHANGE

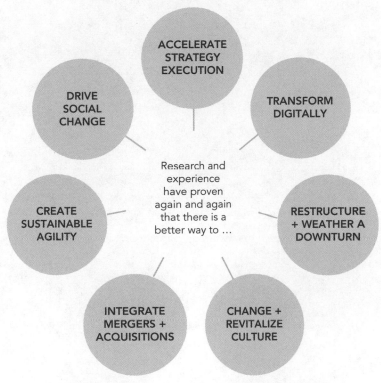

ACCELERATE STRATEGY EXECUTION

TRANSFORM DIGITALLY

DRIVE SOCIAL CHANGE

Research and experience have proven again and again that there is a better way to ...

RESTRUCTURE + WEATHER A DOWNTURN

CREATE SUSTAINABLE AGILITY

INTEGRATE MERGERS + ACQUISITIONS

CHANGE + REVITALIZE CULTURE

AND IN THE END... IT'S ALL ABOUT MORE LEADERSHIP.

A note to all readers: Part II of this book devotes a chapter to each of the methods shown above in the diagram. If you are deeply engaged in one of the methodologies shown in that exhibit and are pressed for time, we suggest you next read the chapter on that method and the last two chapters of the book. You can then decide when and how to engage with the rest of the material.

Part II

THERE IS A BETTER WAY TO ACCELERATE:

Chapter 3

"Strategic Planning" That Delivers Results

No single innovation in the past half century has done more to help organizations and their employees pay attention to complex changes going on around them, and then to adapt intelligently and grow prosperously, than strategy formulation and execution—typically called "strategic planning."

In his seminal history of the whole concept of strategy, Walter Kiechel quotes a BCG consultant circa 1970 as saying "strategy is change." That is, the successful creation and execution of a new strategy inevitably brings changes to a firm, and sometimes an industry—changes that could put an enterprise in a much stronger competitive position relative to others. So, as BCG's founder, Bruce Henderson, would have said, if you believe continuing to operate as you always have is good enough, or you are only willing to make small adjustments, forget thinking about strategy, because a successful strategy exercise almost inevitably leads to change, sometimes significant change.

Back then, this idea was as original as was the whole concept of applying the term "strategy" to the business world, which was what Henderson did, even before Professor Michael Porter launched the idea in academia.

Before that, for centuries, "strategy" was used almost exclusively in the military. By the 1960s, a combination of factors was beginning to produce more competition worldwide, especially for leading organizations in the United States. And strategy—an idea that had proved its usefulness in the ultimate competitive environment of war—began to be developed as a business idea by Porter, Henderson, and a handful of others.

As a new concept in business, strategy caught on relatively quickly. Although few people seem to have made the connection back then, it was in fact a promising methodology to generate needed internal change in the modern organization (that does not change easily) to respond to more external changes emerging at the time.

But today, 50 years later, strategy, as it has come to be employed, is increasingly struggling to keep up as an effective agent of change to promote growth in revenues, profits, or any crucial goal. It often inadvertently ignites too much Survive and too little Thrive. Plugged into the modern organizational form, it is frequently too siloed and bureaucratic. It can violate all known leading change principles: employing a group of drivers that is too small and homogeneous; epitomizing a 90% head and 10% heart, have-to without much want-to process; and too often focusing on crises or problems and not opportunities.

Most of all, strategic planning is very much a management-centric activity, not a leadership-centric activity. Thus it is built on processes designed primarily for reliability and efficiency. As the science of change would predict, it is therefore increasingly incapable of inducing sufficient speed, agility, smart adaptation, and real results that more and more people and institutions need.

An All-Too-Common Strategy Story

A few years ago, a large healthcare system, like most similar systems, was living in a world of increasing cost pressures, reimbursement shifts, and medical science revolutions. Threats and opportunities were growing and were seemingly everywhere. This system had the additional challenge of being the product of a series of acquisitions that were never truly integrated at headquarters or at the level of the hospitals.

At the same time, all was hardly gloomy. The organization had some world-class staff, a few hospitals with national or international reputations, and other assets. The company was run by a relatively new CEO who, along with some on the executive staff, saw new opportunities for growth. They were looking, at least partially, at acquisitions, and for possibilities outside their geographic area or even outside the United States, although there was no consensus on how much or how best to achieve this expansion.

Spurred on by the CEO, the CFO, and a few others, top management began thinking more boldly in their strategic planning. The subsequent discussion was framed through the lens of their current business requirements, their system's four-part mission statement, and their aspirations to take advantage of opportunities conceivably available in their arena. While the organization was known for top-tier research and patient care—which they thought could fuel growth and help patients in other locales—among other strategic issues they identified a need for an unprecedented cost reduction to provide affordable care to patients across their region, fund growth initiatives, and ensure the system would be economically viable over the next decade.

The company engaged a strategy consultancy, which gathered extensive data over a six-month period, looking at decision rights, operating models, revenue sources, operational costs, IT needs, and more. The consultants presented multiple hyper-detailed and very quantitative PowerPoint decks (think 100+ slides) to the executive team and some other senior staff, focusing on the most immediate and the most easily measurable of the issues: cost reduction. Expenses quickly solidified as strategic priority number one (and many insiders would later say "number two, three, four, and five," crowding out other and bigger aspirations). Guided by the strategic consultants, the CEO, hospital leaders, and PMO office identified thirteen areas to focus on ("workstreams"). Each were given target cost savings and an executive "champion" charged with pulling together a small team to execute the work.

When top executives talked about this effort, they highlighted the data and logic behind the changes that would come from the workstreams. Delivered at leadership team meetings and senior functional retreats, this communication reached a few hundred managers and executives (a very small percentage of the total employee population). Metrics were relentlessly tracked and reported to the teams and senior staff involved in the effort. While the work was framed within the context of the opportunity to provide more accessible, affordable, and leading-edge healthcare to current and future communities served, more often than not the "lead" story was only on very measurable cost cutting.

A year and a half into this effort, the system had made some progress in hitting the large cost-cutting goal but they were nowhere near on track to achieve that target in their initial timeframe. Multiple hospitals had laid off employees to help reach their targets, leaving remaining employees fearful that more rounds of layoffs would be coming. Little progress had been made in expanding their footprint or services, and media coverage suggested little movement in terms of reputation in the community.

The whole process caused a growing distrust among much of the staff, at least partly due to lack of transparency and engagement. This led to hesitation in providing data to workstream champions, because it was unclear how the data would be used and what the consequences would be for missing targets. And many employees felt a deep sense of overheated Survive, often sharing in quiet conversations that the change was being done *to* them, rather than *with* them. This made them feel like they were just "waiting for the other shoe to drop." Under these conditions, focus on short-term personal threats went up, as did passive resistance to the whole strategic planning activity.

More complex issues that demanded trust, innovation, or outside-the-hierarchy collaboration achieved little traction, despite pressure or encouragement from a few key executives. The lack of traction undermined the building of momentum. At one point, a frustrated CEO, preparing for a senior management meeting, said, "We cannot trot out that one [innovative, cross-hospital] example again. The people at the meeting have probably heard it five times already."

Senior leaders were not oblivious to much of what was happening. They would privately acknowledge that although progress was being made, they were nowhere near where they needed to be. But having never dealt with such sweeping change at that scale in such a short time frame, they were uncertain what else to do and relied heavily on the consultant's strategic planning methodology, with an emphasis on program management, analytics, and small focused teams.

Eventually, some senior staff began to openly question whether more effort was needed. Others debated the comparative cost data provided by the strategy consultants. Several frustrated leaders willingly left the organization. And some evidence began to emerge that the top five people in management were not on the same page as far as this strategic exercise, which continued to grind on in its own PowerPoint-driven way.

As we write this, the healthcare system in this case has incurred large COVID-19-related costs, wiping out painfully created savings. The system is also in the position of needing to invest hundreds of millions of dollars in new technology and new infrastructure, putting it at risk of ending up with the same challenging cost situation it had five years ago. It has a new CEO.

Some progress has been made at taking advantage of the many potential possibilities in better care, innovative research, and more efficient operations. But compared to lofty hopes and aspirations for strategically using their many human and other assets to build a more integrated system, to avoid wasting precious dollars, and to broaden their impact, these successes seem sadly modest.

Increasingly, individual enterprises and the world at large cannot accept "sadly modest."

The Reigning Method of Change Used in Strategy Formulation and Execution

Although it may never have been made entirely explicit, for easy-to-understand reasons (more on that later), the same methodology for change through strategy formulation and execution came to be employed by most organizations as well as strategy consulting firms. That methodology certainly is present in the above story of the healthcare system. The first step in achieving better outcomes is understanding what this method is, why it came about, and, most fundamentally, why it does not produce needed results in the context we experience more and more today.

This strategy method is based on three basic propositions:

1. It's almost all about top management making smart choices.

2. It's almost all about data and analytics.

3. Most of all, at its core it relies mostly on management, not leadership, but with a longer-term lens—hence strategic planning, reorganizing if structure does not fit strategy, monitoring strategy execution with metrics and other controls.

According to this point of view, change is successful when the most senior management of the relevant unit (total organization, division, country, department) makes very smart choices and then executes those choices very well. Others can obviously play some role, especially in execution, but the only people of *key* importance (the people who will make the decisions and make sure they are implemented) are the top 1% of the total population, or .1%, or (in very large firms) .01%.

Second, according to this methodology, change will be successful when top management operates a multistep process with sophistication and skill. And the process is mostly about data, analytics, and deep thinking to make critical decisions. The steps are typically these:

- Get clarity around the focus. Sometimes the answer to this basic question will be obvious. If the focus is not obvious, the process starts with data gathering, analytical work, and thinking deeply.

- Find the best possible data within the area of focus to give you the basis for really understanding what is going on there.

- Crunch and analyze the data using the latest credible models and methods. If at all possible, use comparative data in the analysis (e.g. average margins in your industry, "benchmarks," "best practices").

- Bring relevant perspectives, experiences, and high-level IQ to bear to absorb the analysis and to set the stage for making smart choices, particularly about what strategic initiatives need to be launched.

- Plan for execution. Will you need to reorganize, move people around, hire in new talent, or add temporary task forces? Will training some people in how to work with the new strategy or culture or quality process be necessary? Do key initiatives need an executive sponsor, and, if yes, who? And so on.

- Execute the plan. Chop the plan into parts and give each piece to the appropriate executive/department/business/plant, and/or to a PMO, perhaps with a "change management" component. Then it's about following through.

The third aspect of this change-through-strategy theory is that strategic change should be driven by management processes. The time frame may be longer than in daily or monthly operational management. The planning itself is a more turbocharged process, with more sophisticated data and analysis. Some additional options are in scope with strategic changes that are not aligned with operational management, such as significant hierarchical shifts, including the creation of whole new departments, divisions, or area structures. While operational metrics and controls tend to be pretty standardized, sometimes new measures must be created to track a novel strategy's implementation. But the key point is that measures are very central to the process.

And unlike leadership, it is almost all about head and little about heart.

Why This Method?

To a large degree, people have used this methodology because it is what naturally evolved given the nature of modern organizations and human hardwiring. It really is a pumped-up version of what executives have done all the time in the modern organizational form, starting a century and a half ago. That is, they manage through hierarchy, controls, and policies. So what was already well known and thoroughly built into organizations was just adjusted to include more data, more analytics, a longer planning horizon, and more sophisticated project management execution.

In terms of human nature, the core of the process that actually produces change—the execution phase—is all about finding and solving problems. That fits comfortably with the dominant Survive Channel in our brains/bodies. That is, it asks people what they are inclined to do by ancient hardwiring.

And while human nature is not dominated by high analytic thinking, a number of powerful forces have aided organizations to make up for this deficit in natural ability. Aids include the huge evolution of computer power, the accumulation of massive data sets on industries and countries, an explosion in business school education, and the ever-growing management consulting industry staffed by analytically sophisticated business school graduates.

Flaws in the Methodology

As a concept for how to create effective change through strategic planning, this method always had some limitations. In today's faster-moving and more multifaceted world, the limitations are only growing more and more serious.

The first part of the process—strategy work driven entirely by top management—presents multifold problems.

- Trying to run everything through a very busy and relatively small executive team inevitably leads to decisions being made too slowly, especially in a more rapidly moving world. Or top managers are forced to make quick decisions, the implications of which they inevitably do not fully understand.

- We know from research that when change occurs faster and in more perplexing ways, with more interdependencies across regions, units, and functions, a small group of individuals will find it increasingly difficult to have all the necessary information to make effective decisions. When large-scale change is successful, especially in a swiftly changing world, significant numbers of reasonably unknown people sometimes become especially important. These diverse groups are closer to products, customers, technology, or internal processes. They may be far from the executive committee, but in a better position to spot threats and opportunities that highlight a need to revisit strategy, offer new and more relevant ideas, and provide leadership that makes important action happen fast enough.

Net, net: the notion that it is all about the top executives fits comfortably within the logic of the modern managerial-centric organization but does not necessarily lead to successful strategy formulation or implementation in a rapidly changing context that demands leadership.

The second part of strategy's current change methodology implicitly says that the overwhelming key to success is getting the data and analytics right and interpreting them correctly. It is all about thinking clearly, deeply, and systemically—and the best data is usually "hard," not soft, because more rigorous analysis can be done with numbers.

This belief, of course, flies in the face of the research on complex change, the reality of human nature, and today's more swiftly moving world. For example, in one substantial study of nearly 100 big change initiatives, among the 20 judged to be most successful, the number where data and analysis—versus experiences and feelings—were the key to success was *zero*. That is not to say that, in the grade A cases, data and deep thinking were missing. Most of the time the quality of the thinking was very good. But in terms of being the core force making the change happen successfully and swiftly, something else was obviously in play, something more associated with hearts than heads. (For more on this, see the Notes at the end of the book.)

And even pre-execution, the standard strategy model assumes that you can get a sufficient amount of the right data for making projections considerably into the future. This ignores today's reality that as the speed and complexity of change increases, our capacity to make big predictions into the future declines. Such is the nature of heightened uncertainty. Think COVID-19.

The third part of the method—strategic change as a variation on traditional managerial processes—was somewhat off 40 years ago and is much more wrong today. As we have described before, management processes were designed to produce reliable, repeatable performance, not change. The method of working through hierarchy and controls cannot begin to gather and process enough of the right sorts of information fast enough to create viable strategic plans in a 100-mile-per-hour world of curving roads nearly everywhere.

With the traditional process, the "planning" piece of strategic planning tends to prescribe in more and more detail how to achieve the goals. Consequently, this restricts the degrees of freedom and room for innovation that employees have during implementation. The one-and-done nature of traditional strategy, dictated by the calendar once a year at most, also hampers innovation, as anyone who has worked in successful startups knows, since in that context people change strategies in reaction to market feedback all the time.

Modern organizations have a built-in tendency to "cascade" plans down through the hierarchy, a process that cannot begin to activate Thrive to the degree needed in enough people to overcome all the barriers to strategic change. Activating Thrive requires people to see opportunities and not just threats, and if those people do not have some engagement as the plans are being formulated, the Survive Channel's natural fear of the unknown kicks in. People see changes as a threat to their jobs, status, or egos.

Furthermore, the controls so central to management and the modern organization actually constrain more than they energize in a positive way. The change management techniques that are founded on this theory focus on controlling the change through information dissemination, formal processes, and top-down mandates, with very little focus on people and the human nature that is largely responsible for how individuals respond to change.

Some people who intuitively see how management through hierarchy can suppress much-needed Thrive activation have labeled it a leftover from the past and have argued that leadership through networks is the future. But this idea misses a fundamental point. Both are needed because they serve different purposes: reliability, efficiency, standardization, and stability for management; innovation, mobilization, adaptation, and change for leadership. As the pace and complexity of change accelerates, the quotient of leadership has to increase. And, as we shall discuss more fully later, research shows that more from more people is possible.

Strategy as a Mobilizing Agent to Get *Results*

Around the same time that the strategy story told earlier in this chapter was unfolding, a health tech company also embarked on a strategic planning process. They were smaller, which is usually a change advantage. But the challenges they faced were just as significant, if not more so—especially around a frustrating inability to figure out and execute a path to growth in a dynamic marketplace, where lots of change meant many growth options existed. Indeed, every one of their competitors was outgrowing them. Their lack of revenue increases meant constant pressure on costs, losses of market share, stagnant share price, and a perilous future.

Just as in the first story, top management performed a market analysis looking at global trends as well as their position in the market. Through this analysis, senior executives knew some areas of their business were missing the mark, which was having significant impact on top- and bottom-line financials. But they took a very different approach to *how* they finalized and executed their strategy.

The leaders of the organization decided there was a unique opportunity to drive growth through acquisitions, better integration of past acquisitions, improved processes and products, and market expansion—*"powered by the many."* That is, their concept was that engaged and mobilized employees would be the key to ultimately driving top- and bottom-line growth. Top management's view was that their job was to provide the leadership that would empower others to lead, and that strategic change would be more an exercise in vision, alignment, and inspiration (leadership) than planning, hierarchy, and controls (management). Although not 100% of the top team bought in, the idea of engaged volunteers leading unprecedented change was explained in a convincing enough way that it was eventually embraced by most.

Senior executives aligned themselves around a compelling description of a big opportunity for the firm, its employees, its customers, and even public health. Management shared this regularly with everyone, not just with the top of the hierarchy. This statement was crafted to be ambitious, but not *rah-rah* unreal. It painted a picture of the future that, we have been told many times by many of their employees, successfully engaged people's hearts and minds and tapped into their desire to want to help create this future. Furthermore, it highlighted the strengths that the organization could lean on to achieve the vision. It fit on one PowerPoint slide. Initiatives were then prioritized based on their ability to help achieve both this opportunity and the organization's strategic goals.

Diverse teams were created, leveraging both subject matter experts (SMEs) and energized volunteers from across different parts and layers of the organization. Supported by executive sponsors, who committed to remove barriers when needed and then get out of the way (no micromanaging), these teams were given space to decide how to achieve key initiative goals and were expected to engage employees across the entire business, which they did.

With this approach, energy and excitement began to grow. Some results came quickly because they targeted certain initiatives to gain credibility. Successes—even small ones—were identified, celebrated, and *broadly* communicated. Cross-silo collaboration increased because of diverse teams and because of a low level of Survive-induced silo mentality. With it, innovation started to be unleashed in ways the organization had not seen before.

When big financial metrics visible to the public did not quickly change, this led to two challenging quarters and some internal consternation about the path they were on. Those who had never fully bought in raised question after question. But some strong voices on the executive committee pointed out that logical leading indicators (e.g. number of "volunteers," number of new ideas) were moving in the right direction. This bought them time in which they were able to hold the course.

And it paid off. The organization began growing for the first time in years and became an industry leader across multiple metrics. According to employees and their bosses, the firm's culture evolved, creating a more innovative, collaborative, high-speed, fun, and purposeful place to work.

Some metrics that capture the changes are:

- From little to no growth, sales increases jumped dramatically to 25% per year, year after year, which was unprecedented.

- Stock price tripled in less than three years. This was unparalleled except for one time in their earliest days.

- Employee engagement scores rose enough to take them from industry laggard to industry leader to highest ever recorded in their industry.

- Annualized turnover decreased four percentage points, which translated into significant dollars saved.

- Valued employee retention increased (a small percentage shift but one that had a considerable impact).

- Two-thirds of the organization raised their hands to be part of a "volunteer army," literally choosing to make themselves available to work on strategic projects "without time off from your regular job"—another totally unprecedented occurrence.

- Three-quarters of this "volunteer army" was actively involved in strategic projects each month, so this resource was more than a theoretical asset mostly sitting in a "warehouse." And these projects regularly achieved staggering results.

- The CEO said publicly on many occasions that these results, in total, would have seemed "unimaginable" to virtually all executives and other employees at the beginning of their "transformational journey."

All the data we have in this situation (and because we were involved in the story we have a great deal of data) suggest the CEO is not overstating the case one bit.

A Better Method in a Rapidly Shifting World

How did the company in the second story produce real results that were so much more dramatic, swift, and transformational than the firm in the first? The answer is clear, and it fits the messages from the emerging science of change. Simply put, it is a leadership-centric approach to strategy, not a management-centric approach.

This superior approach starts with the premise that what we typically ask executive committees to do today in strategy formulation and execution is an increasingly impossible task. This method recognizes that to deal with all the barriers to change, at the pace needed, without inadvertently overheating Survive, you need diverse masses dedicated to helping you lead change. That means people from all the relevant departments and staff from the top to the bottom of the organization.

Creating and sustaining this broad level of engagement, participation, and leadership is not possible without activating many peoples' Thrive Channel and the associated feelings of excitement, passion, and purpose. Without a significant group of engaged bodies and brains, without large numbers of alert eyeballs (and activated opportunity-seeking radars), it simply is not possible to see all the most relevant changes happening in the product marketplace, the labor and financial markets, the surrounding communities, and within key governments. Without enough sufficiently engaged people actually providing some leadership, it is not possible to overcome all the barriers to strategic change inside modern organizations in a timely manner. There is too much information, too many people to influence, too much needed communication, and of course too many people and policies and silos that can block sensible strategic change.

A BETTER APPROACH TO STRATEGY
IN AN ERA OF RAPID CHANGE

MANAGEMENT-CENTRIC APPROACH TO STRATEGY	LEADERSHIP-CENTRIC APPROACH TO STRATEGY
Strategy execution focuses on creating robust plans, metrics, taskforces, budgets, timelines, etc., with an aim to provide efficient and reliable implementation.	Robust implementation *management* is supported by active, visible *leadership* that inspires, motivates, and creates intellectual and emotional buy-in throughout the organization with an aim to foster innovation and adaptability, in addition to reliability and efficiency.
Often framed as a response to a threat, as a "burning platform." Even growth opportunities are often framed as "what happens if we miss this window." Connection to company mission is often unclear or unarticulated.	Always framed as a response to both threats and the available opportunities. "What can be achieved when we are successful." Clearly articulated link to company mission.
Relies on an elite *select few*, not only to analyze information and make decisions, but also to execute the strategy.	Engages *diverse many* in providing information/insights in the strategy formulation process and even more so in leading execution.
Successfully activates Survive and compels *"have-to"* action from people.	Successfully activates Survive and Thrive and inspires *"want-to"* action in addition to compelling *"have-to"* action.
The benefits of the strategy are communicated through rational, analytical arguments that speak to the *head*.	The impact of the strategy is communicated through both metrics that speak to the *head* and a vision of success that speaks to the *heart*.

Most people, especially in big organizations, have never seen such a large-scale leadership-centric strategy process. So executives often logically believe this Thrive-oriented approach only creates chaos, conflict, or distraction from getting their daily routine jobs done well. They are inclined to wonder if the idea is "theory" and impractical, or only suited to some limited situations. We know through research and much personal experience that it is not. In the following chapters we will share more stories of companies that have been able to execute against their strategies and achieve outstanding results through this leadership-centric approach.

For some organizations, strategic planning as a simple extension of a budgeting process, or as a souped-up version of management generally, will not create disaster anytime soon because they are in a safe harbor or are in some way in an exceptionally strong position relative to competitors.

But think about the potential consequences of continuing to handle strategy in the all-too-common management-centric way.

If We Don't Change Our Approach to Strategy

Already we are beginning to see places where life moves fast enough that the linear managerial steps in traditional strategy formulation and strategy execution start to bleed into each other. Execution produces new data needed in analysis. Waiting until an entire design is done, as opposed to starting to execute plans as soon as they are off the drawing board, so to speak, slows you down. Or you get caught in a never-ending, interrupted dynamic. So, halfway through design, something changes that has a material effect on the analysis, which stops you and sends you back to analysis. Or, during execution, you learn something that shows a key design decision is now wrong, sending you back again.

It is possible to employ a leadership-centric approach to strategic planning in this sort of world using a process similar to our second strategy story—and with dramatic results. It demands competent senior management, but not larger-than-life leaders. As in the health tech story, it can produce results that benefit people broadly—investors, customers, employees, and more—and help them to a degree that will seem to many "unimaginable" at first.

Chapter 4

Digital Transformation That Is Truly Transformational

Perhaps more than any other single force, the so-called digital revolution is changing the world in ways that are creating threats and opportunities for organizations everywhere. And in response, digital transformation is to some degree going on all around us, as an organizational change initiative both to minimize threats and to maximize the chances of gaining opportunity.

What digital transformation can do to accelerate major change was on full display during the period March–May 2020. Those among us who were lucky enough, smart enough, or positioned well enough used digital to make some major changes faster and more fundamentally, in a shorter period of time, than almost anyone thought possible—working from home being the most dramatic example.

There seem to be a number of key actions, all logical in light of the emerging science of change, that create "the impossible" through digital transformation. But, as you will soon see, none are more central than the appropriate application of the principle of select few *and* diverse many.

Digital transformation driven by a select few is the norm today. Add diverse many to the playbook and the amount, speed, and effectiveness of change can go up dramatically.

The Digital Revolution

Digital transformation takes many increasingly familiar forms. For retail, it is the replacement of physical stores with curated, online shopping. In health care, it is partly telehealth, which offers the promise of far more efficient access to top-notch medical care. For manufacturing businesses, it is the promise of industry 4.0 and, for example, equipment that is connected and that can send alerts when maintenance is required. For large organizations nearly everywhere, it is a vast information infrastructure that efficiently handles accounting, financial reporting, engineering analyses, sales forecasting, monitoring of plans and communication to managers, screening resumes, and much, much more. For the newspaper, magazine, and book business, it is the transformation of the industries' products themselves from a traditional form to a whole new entity. It is at the heart of artificial intelligence (AI), the Internet of Things (IoT), machine learning, cloud enablement, e-learning, and more.

Digital transformation is a direct response to one of the most fundamental changes of our time: the movement from the Industrial Age to the Information Age. And it is happening at unprecedented speed. Hunting and gathering societies around the globe evolved and lasted over a hundred thousand years. The transition to agricultural societies took thousands of years. The transition from agricultural to industrial societies took a few hundred years. Starting with some noticeable thrust in the 1980s, the movement toward an Information Age is taking decades.

SPEED OF CHANGE

ERA	Hunting + Gathering Societies	Agricultural Societies	Industrial Societies	Information/ Knowledge Societies
SPEED OF CHANGE WITHIN ERA	Very, very slow	Mostly slow	Much faster than before	Faster all the time
LASTED	100,000+ years	10,000+ years	100s of years	Just starting

Though digitally-driven change is much more frequent, powerful, and noticeable in some contexts than others, it is hard to find a place where digitization is not being used to cope with change, if only of total necessity.

Understanding the Digital Transformation Challenge in Organizations

The people who have most directly benefited from the use of digital transformation tend to see its success rate as high. Or certainly not low. Researchers with less to gain or lose from studying success rates tend to be more critical—less so of its necessity or promise and more so of its current methodology and results. In particular, serious investigations point to budget-busting costs, irritating delays, useless disruption, and unrealized benefits.

Sometimes the promises being chased are unrealistic. Much more often, the problems encountered look very much like the challenges you find derailing strategy exercises (and, as you will shortly see, restructuring, cultural revitalization, and M&A).

Study digital transformations that fail, and you often find a lack of clarity about *why* the transformation is being undertaken and what opportunities the business will realize from the complex changes. Digital transformation can refer to many different things from a software implementation that makes operations more efficient to the development of an omnichannel retail strategy to establishing new products or offerings. Without a clear description of what you hope to achieve, the efforts can quickly drive up a collective sense of anxiety and dissolve into disconnected projects that overheat Survive and don't move the business forward.

Part of the problem here is that digital transformations are also particularly susceptible to a "jump on the bandwagon" approach, with the temptation of new and exciting technologies and innovations. Companies that resist this temptation and approach digital within the context of a business objective are far more successful.

For example, when Best Buy was faced with competition from Amazon and the threat of "showrooming" (the practice of checking out products in a physical store but ordering the item at a discount online), it responded by reevaluating the customer experience. This highlighted some advantages that were masquerading as disadvantages, thus finding opportunity, even in the midst of challenge.

Best Buy was able to reconfigure its supply chain and leverage its retail footprint to offer the service of ordering online to pick up in store. Additionally, by transforming its view of its vendors, Best Buy saw an opportunity to use its outlets as a showroom (for which they charged "rent") for the products of manufacturers like Apple, Microsoft, Google, and yes, even Amazon. These changes required a better online presence, mobile apps, and integrated inventory systems, but these digital enhancements were implemented within the context of the broader business strategy.

The failure to have clear integration of digital and business strategy arises easily when digital and business units are not integrated organizationally. We see this all the time.

The modern organizational form groups activities into silos, and digital transformation efforts are often "managed" by small, highly trained, very "head-dominated" people in an IT department or some other digital enclave. A somewhat extreme example would be GE, which in 2015 formed a separate business unit, GE Digital, with the aim to centralize all IT operations of the business and to establish a "software development" unit. GE recognized significant opportunities in Industry 4.0 and wanted to be a leader in the Industrial Internet of Things. The goal of establishing GE Digital as a separate unit with its own P&L was to create a revenue-generating unit. However, GE Digital was also the avenue for the other business units to enable their own digital transformations.

For a large conglomerate like GE, each business unit had very different digital needs. By centralizing the digital transformation, and doing little to inspire people to want to collaborate and innovate across silos, this led to a disconnect between digital transformation initiatives and business unit objectives and opportunities. This failure to integrate GE Digital and to scale the benefits across the business is reflected in the decision to spin it off as an independently operated business.

When businesses embark on a digital transformation in order to replicate the success of industry-disrupting startups, it is often easier and hence tempting to create separate digital business units. We have seen this mistake before in the context of innovation; think Xerox Parc. By not integrating your digital ambitions with your core business, you might create some innovative new offerings, but it will not transform your core business, which is fast becoming a necessity for nearly everyone.

The Problem with Data

Digital transformations tend to create more data. For the most part today, this increase in information and data is seen as an asset, and not as both an asset and a problem.

More information is generally viewed as good, essential, and even more promising now with artificial intelligence, machine learning, and those big data methodologies. Given the nature of management, which is so central to the modern organization, there is a natural bias in this direction. The saying "You cannot manage what you cannot measure" is but one reason there is such a halo around "data."

Yet along with the many benefits, virtually *all* spreadsheets, monthly budget updates, customer satisfaction surveys, employee engagement or morale or attitude surveys, dashboards, project management updates, market research studies, industry statistics, strategic analyses—you name it—bring some news that research has shown the brain can view as threatening. And as that news increases with more and more data, those perceived threats can send us into an overstressed, low-innovation state, associated with an overheated Survive Channel.

Our hardwiring can sometimes perceive massive amounts of information as threatening because it reveals that we are not entirely on plan, because a number is not as good as in the last report, or because something is less than the boss has said she expects. Data can be perceived as threatening because the projection for the possible future for our services falls below our hopes, hurting our division or department. Or it's threatening because the sheer volume available, without a clear sense of how to best leverage it, is overwhelming.

The human hardwiring that evolved very long ago for a very different kind of threat—generally physical ones—is not very good at distinguishing between the important, significant threats in the data and the mild (or nonexistent) ones. Our internal systems can treat all this "negative" data just as if we had spotted a predator in the bush. Too many threats then overheat Survive, which can make it less effective and can slow down Thrive or even shut it down completely.

How often does this sort of data-driven threat assault managers? We have tried actually counting. For one middle manager at a midsize-to-large energy company, email attachments, old-fashioned paper reports, PowerPoint decks in meetings, customer surveys, financial updates, project timeline updates, reports from regulatory agencies, sales forecasts created by AI and big data (the list seemed endless) all added up to three sets of reports per week, each containing a minimum of 200–1,000 numbers. At the low end, that equals 2,400 potential pieces of bad news a month. In a really *good* organization (and this manager's was by most standards good), perhaps 90% of the news is actually positive, showing that we are on target today or that we have new opportunities in the future. But the remaining 10% leaves us with 240 threats!

And this does not take into account an avalanche of information that assaults us from our computers and smartphones, search engines, social media, cable TV, as well as our ability to manipulate reports to look at multiple scenarios. When you consider that, the 240 can triple, or even multiply much more.

The biggest issue of all is the fact that so few people even recognize the data explosion that comes with digital transformation as a problem in all these ways, or talk about this as a serious issue.

Our point here is not that big data is bad (it clearly is not) or that digital transformation is not extremely important (it certainly is). Our point is that the norm today, again for understandable reasons given the nature of modern organizations, easily misses the data-brain problem and thus can push us down a path that slows or undermines needed change. And there is a vastly better alternative that can transform—which you need to embrace as soon as possible.

An SAP Implementation That Worked

Seemingly every large organization has a story of a disappointing ERP (enterprise resource planning) or CRM (customer relationship management) software implementation. A lack of controls, management oversight, or technical challenges are the most cited reasons for these less-than-ideal implementations. Given the scale and complexity of these implementations, it is no surprise that the challenges we are describing in this book are felt even more acutely.

What you repeatedly find are small and homogeneous (often elite) groups guiding the effort, without being aided by diverse and massive numbers of people providing energy, urgency, enthusiasm, knowledge, and connections to others. You also find people appointed to do the work and precious few others essentially volunteering to help because they want the work done well and their hearts are in it. You find a traditional management process, heavy on plans, linear movement, metrics, policy, hierarchy, and controls. You don't find a lighter-touch management working with either Thrive-activating leadership coming from all the relevant silos or an initiative that is not dependent on hierarchy. And with that approach, you find a set of change-oriented tasks that, given the nature of modern enterprises, run into countless organizational barriers.

Simply put, you encounter once again an approach that woefully underactivates Thrive. And, to a degree generally unrecognized, you find an overactivated Survive keeping Thrive down.

Highly positive and successful SAP implementation stories are rare. As a general rule, older industries struggle even more with digitization, which is why we love this story.

The firm involved is an electric and water utility, the origins of which go back more than a century. It is located in Europe, in a region with a deep history. The utility serves millions of customers in its geographic area.

In a bold move made by a bold CEO, the firm embarked on a digital transformation that involved a radical review of the entire business operations: from the organizational structure and processes; to the relationship with customers; to the way information flowed through the organization. The firm decided not just to upgrade their primitive digital infrastructure but essentially to skip one whole technological generation and go from pencil and paper to electronic notebooks for field staff, a change so profound it necessitated a new company logo.

Workers for generations would show up at dispatch, have coffee with their colleagues, and then walk regular routes, often seeing familiar faces. No more. With this upgrade, they would now wake up to an iPad setting their most efficient route for the day.

This software upgrade was clearly connected to a broader business strategy, with the utility looking to move from a slow, top-down decision-making model to one that was faster and closer to the customer. The digital transformation was a critical component of achieving a new vision of creating the first utility in the region to recognize and respond to customers who had already changed habits, needs, and expectations. A successful digital transformation of this sort could embolden the organization—or so they were told by experts—to go beyond a sleepy monopoly to a model for their industry in customer responsiveness, efficiency, and business performance. The ramifications could be huge: for the government, the population, employees, the workplace, and more.

Given the scale of the ambition, top management decided not to use simple and limited software but instead opted for a comprehensive installation of SAP, which could enable incredible efficiencies and allow them to think differently about both how they deployed resources and how they managed customer relationships.

In launching the transformation, the leadership team was made acutely aware of the potential to unnecessarily trigger the employees' Survive Channel. They therefore communicated transparently and consistently, even acknowledging that the digitization effort would eliminate some roles and that the changes to end-to-end processes would require significant changes in how work was done. Leadership also communicated their goal to create new productive roles for all their employees and hence avoid layoffs.

Additionally, a case for change was crafted that high-lighted why the transformation was being undertaken, the opportunities the organization could take advantage of, why they were well positioned to do so, and why now was the right time. This opportunity statement, which was designed to speak to both the head and the heart, was treated not as one more piece of paper with corporate-speak but as a Thrive activating rallying cry for the organization.

A comprehensive implementation of SAP under the most agreeable circumstances is no small feat, and the transformation effort did run into challenges. But utilizing many of the strategies described in this book, the company was able to overcome these and make rapid progress.

One of the first initiatives was inspired by a very basic problem. With the clock ticking on a transformation schedule, the executive committee was repeatedly told that their huge customer database had at least 150,000 missing or obviously inaccurate fields. Further, they were informed that a prerequisite for the SAP implementation was an accurate and clean data set. And, they were told, they had no capacity inside the utility to do such a cleanup job in any reasonable time frame.

Someone approached a number of qualified vendors. The need was explained: fill in the missing, incomplete, or obviously wrong information on names of customers, addresses, water/electric usage, and accounts receivable. Get the work done quickly to keep the project on sched-ule. Only one firm even responded. Their message was simple and clear: "No one can possibly do what you are asking within the time frame required."

The case for change as articulated in the opportunity statement had been presented to a broader employee audience. The leadership team had utilized some theatrics to make the message emotionally compelling by, for example, creating a moment of complete darkness to represent the unsettling nature of change. Although not everyone jumped on board immediately, some employees did instantly like the concept. So a team of neutral or positive responders was assembled from people in all ranks and departments. This group was given permission to use their imagination around how to create a sense of urgency throughout the organization about the opportunity to develop a new kind of utility.

This team was guided in how to challenge employees to view change as an act of freedom, and a way to build a stronger and more dynamic, modern company. With sufficient success in finding people whose thinking resonated with this message, a clean-up-the-data initiative was immediately organized and staffed entirely by volunteers. This group obtained information by contacting customers on evenings and weekends. They combed through municipalities area by area, block by block, and home by home, in order to get an address, a phone number, a counter reading—everything they needed. They literally demolished walls in order to find hidden electric and water meters. Individuals reported finding equipment buried beneath or behind construction, as well as equipment hidden from view by overgrown bushes. This labor-intensive effort could never have been completed without Thrive-activated employees working on a task that was not part of their job descriptions.

As the missing or known-to-be-incorrect data was replaced with accurate information at a swifter than expected pace, enthusiasm and effort grew. Before a self-imposed, ambitious 90-day clock ran out, all 150,000 data fields were filled in with precise information: names, addresses, usage, and so on.

To the total astonishment of many, including some on the executive committee, the SAP implementation moved forward on schedule and on budget.

This "it cannot be done" success pulled in more employees who wanted to be engaged in the process, as articulated in their "opportunity statement." Many lined up wanting to use the new technology, as opposed to feeling it was being forced on them.

More initiatives were launched. One focused on collecting unpaid bills—unpaid because they did not have accurate customer data before, so that many invoices were not even making it to the correct individuals. In a remarkably short period of time, they pulled in 100 million euros (virtually all of which went to operating profit). Another initiative focused on a procurement process for small purchases that took an aggravating 50 days on average, and reduced that typical time to less than 10 days—an outcome which naysayers had said was "totally impossible." Again, and again, diverse, large teams provided heartfelt leadership to overcome endless bureaucratic and other barriers.

An incredibly complex digital technology was successfully implemented, which began leading to some pretty profound business outcomes.

The new actions, better results, communication, and celebration, repeated again and again, began to build a radically different mindset among many employees. Technology and data were perceived less as threats and more as a lubricant for the rapid creation of a whole new level of prosperity. One of the people involved in the initial stages remarked that at the start "it seemed just a fantasy," but witnessing, participating, and celebrating the successes changed the employees on both a personal ("it opened up my mind," someone said) and a professional level.

Employees—most of them, not just a few technical experts—started to believe that not only was formidable change happening faster, and not only did they need to change more and faster in response inside the firm, but that it really was possible.

In this case, watching people in a company in what many would call a dull industry do "the impossible," and then be busting with pride because of that . . . well, it was actually thrilling.

Making Digital Transformation Work

So what did the old-school utility do that led to its success?

WHY ELITE DIGITAL SILOS ALONE DON'T CREATE DIGITAL TRANSFORMATION	HOW DIVERSE MASSES <u>PLUS</u> DIGITAL ELITE DRIVE DIGITAL TRANSFORMATION
Incomplete or unclear business objectives for the transformation	A compelling articulation of what opportunities can be realized through the transformation
Making reactive (to competitors, markets, new technologies) moves that are not integrated with all aspects of the business strategy	An integrated approach that derives all activities from business objectives
Focusing mostly on the technology, and the data, not on people impacted and the adoption of the change	Focusing on behaviors, mindsets, and engagement in addition to tools, technology, and training
Not appreciating or addressing the anxiety, uncertainty, and the avalanche of data caused by the transformation	Address the fears and anxieties of employees—calm the Survive Channel
Engage a small homogeneous group, leading to missed opportunities, limited support, and resistance	Build urgency and commitment from a broad group of employees
Rigid implementation and an overreliance on management processes	Inspire action and leadership by activating the Thrive Channel among a broad employee base

First, they avoided most of the pitfalls that stop digital efforts from being transformational: unclear business objectives, treating it (in this case SAP) as a shiny new ball not really integrated into a broader business strategy, focusing almost solely on technology instead of on people and change, not dealing with the anxiety caused by transformation, relying on small and homogeneous groups to design and implement the work, and a rigid overreliance on management process. Indeed, they did the opposite in almost all of these areas.

They developed a compelling articulation of what opportunities might be realized through the work. They had a business strategy that dictated the activities that were most relevant. They focused on behaviors, mindsets, and engagement in addition to tools, technology, and training. They addressed fears and anxieties (calmed the Survive Channel).

And most of all, they built urgency and commitment, inspired action and leadership, among a broad employee base. They did not try to drive digital transformation through a limited group of technical experts in an IT silo.

And this methodology worked remarkably well, just as the emerging science of accelerated, large-scale change would predict.

Chapter 5

Restructuring Without Killing Innovation and Your Future

"Restructuring" is a significant change to the operational or financial structure of a business in order to improve performance, often by focusing on efficiencies and profitability. Restructuring is accompanied by changes in how business activities and people are organized.

Like strategic planning in general, and digital transformation as one specific sort of strategic change initiative, under the right circumstances restructuring can be a useful methodology for driving needed and beneficial change. Restructuring has probably been used since the emergence of the modern organization over a century ago. During recessions, it has been utilized extensively. But in the last few decades, all available evidence suggests it is being used more and more often.

As we write this, organizations around the world, both public and private, are restructuring more than ever to cope with the effects of COVID-19 and the associated economic downturn. Right now, it looks as if large numbers of small or undercapitalized businesses will not survive. Restructuring will not save them, and in fact may make their problems worse by overheating Survive, killing Thrive, and thus undercutting innovation. This negative impact comes at a time when innovation to address a changing world is essential. If that were not bad enough, best evidence suggests the problem could actually become much bigger.

But it does not have to be this way.

Accomplishing Hard-to-Imagine Results

The emerging science of change shows how traditional restructuring can create serious problems today and how an alternative approach can avoid these problems. A recent case we have been studying shows the upside potential.

A well-known global consumer products enterprise, headquartered in Europe, decided that a significant restructuring of their manufacturing organization was needed. Technological evolutions were making some of their equipment and methods obsolete. Geographic shifts in demand, along with some acquisitions, had led to overcapacity and a far less than ideal manufacturing footprint.

A comprehensive six-month study led the executive committee to the conclusion that small incremental shifts, no matter how clever or innovative, would not restore competitiveness to their supply chain. Something much bigger, and more painful, was necessary. Specifically, they decided to reduce their footprint from 18 factories to 13. Five plants in four different countries would be closed or sold, in total leading to around 2,000 job losses.

Because all the plants were unionized, most had many long-term employees. The company's executives realized that any announcement about shutting down five factories would run into a tidal wave of anger, anxiety, and even depression. It was anticipated that this restructuring would be tense and disruptive. Risks were not insignificant, since strikes, a loss of key personnel who would be needed to make orderly and efficient closures possible, or a general collapse in productivity among alienated people could all have very serious economic ramifications. Yet common sense dictated that to achieve the real goal, profitable growth, manufacturing had to be more competitive and the only way to make that happen within a reasonable time frame was through this restructuring.

The executive they put in charge of the overall project had actually experienced a large-scale change based on the leadership processes and the four principles described in this book. He recommended to the executive committee that his experiences be used to guide their restructuring, customized to fit the details of their situation. His recommendation was initially met with serious skepticism from other top managers who had histories with restructurings and closures that were mostly very unpleasant. "There will be a strike." "You can't trust people under these circumstances." "You shouldn't tell people early or the best ones will leave, hurting our ability to continue operations until shutdown."

He walked top management through what he had seen done before. He gave concrete examples of how large numbers of people could be emotionally engaged in a positive way; of the benefits of helping employees personally see an opportunity for themselves, not just a horrific threat; of leadership coming from a diverse many; of winning hearts and minds; and more.

It was a hard sell. But with sufficient real-world examples, with his commitment to metrics for costs and productivity that the executive committee demanded, they (with reservations) let him proceed with his unconventional approach.

A case for change for the business, as developed by the firm's senior staff, was presented at each plant. These sessions were brief and factual. There was no effort to sugarcoat the situation. Leaders were transparent about the impact of their outdated technology systems and lack of competitive manufacturing footprint—and how they believed the plant closures were absolutely needed to ameliorate the situation. They shared the results of the 6-month study that helped them identify which plants to close and set a clear timeline for what was to come (assuring people they would shut each site in no sooner than 12–15 months).

The short presentation was immediately followed up with longer sessions in smaller groups at each site. In these longer, unscripted meetings, the emotion poured out, sometimes brutally. In a move the audiences certainly did not anticipate, they were told that in addition to the typical metrics of productivity during the restructuring work and incremental shutdown costs, two new measures would be added. They were the answers to two questions that would be asked of all employees just before closure. "First, given the decision to close the plant, which we would never expect you to agree with, were you treated right and fairly? Yes, or no?" Second, "Were you able, with our support, to define your own personal outcome and are you on track to achieve that?" The ultimate goal was to receive positive answers to both questions from an overwhelming percentage of employees.

Some people left these sessions cautiously optimistic, or at least less anxious and angry. Many were still mad, and disbelieving.

A 20-person group in each factory, which came to be called the Works Committee, was constituted to be in charge of making and executing decisions to drive the process. People were told they could put their names forward if they wanted to be considered for the committee. Volunteers came from all levels in the organization, including technicians, middle managers, and senior leaders. Elections were held to choose among the candidates. The percentage of voter turnout at each site was in the high 90s.

Subsequently, all decisions about how to shut these factories down were made by these groups. They did not have any say in whether the plants should be kept open wholly or partially. And they were held accountable for the metrics set by senior management. But, in return, they were given the power to drive the shutdown process, instead of it being driven by remote senior management.

In addition to the usual discussions and decisions that needed to be had and made under these circumstances, the Works Committees held sessions for employees on the emotional cycle people tend to go through in these sorts of major changes (paying attention to "heart" issues as well as "head"). They helped people think about what they would like to do next in their work lives and how they could pursue making that happen. As a result of these meetings, some people decided they wanted to stay in a similar manufacturing world. But some decided to retire, open restaurants, or go back to school. And virtually all appreciated the unanticipated help.

Overwrought anger and anxiety went down a bit.

At all sites, the Works Committees decided to create "change visions." None minced words: the plant will be shut down. But all made commitments to treating employees fairly and well. The committees were responsible for a broad arena of restructuring communications. Most committees generated "buzz" with innovative posters and publicity campaigns whose communication successfully attracted people to volunteer to join them on their journey. And although it was not formally in their charters, all committees celebrated what employees would see as wins, including people who left early because they received terrific job offers.

More and more people (although not all) were won over by the process and the growing trust in the individual running the restructuring. As angst went down, creativity in hitting shutdown metrics went up.

Long story short, when the plants were closed or turned over to new owners:

- Productivity in the final days was as high or higher than it had been before the announcement of the closings, which most of the executive committee had dismissed as impossible.

- Every financial metric set down by top management was met or exceeded, to the delight of top management.

- No productivity had been lost because of work stoppages, strikes, or slowdowns—something else that most of the executive committee had assumed was impossible with the playbook recommended to them and subsequently used.

- Still-needed production was moved to the other remaining plants with minimal or no disruption.

- The smooth and successful closure allowed senior management to avoid many potential distractions and to stay focused on the other activities needed to realize the overall benefits of restructuring.

- 96% of all employees answered yes to the questions about whether they felt they had been treated fairly and well, and whether they were able to define their own personal preferred outcome and were on the way to achieving it. (Perhaps pause a second and let that figure sink in: 96%.)

The Restructuring Challenge

While there are many different reasons to restructure an organization, most fall in one of two camps. The first, in which the ultimate goal of restructuring tends to be greater efficiencies and profitability, has cost cutting as a central focus. Since payroll is such a large budget item for the vast majority of businesses, these restructurings usually involve some layoffs and perhaps even a very large number of layoffs. The second reason, usually triggered by a shift in the internal or external environment, is motivated by the need to change how the business operates and what activities are performed. While this second type of restructuring may not involve significant layoffs, it does require anxiety-inducing realignment of roles and the individuals in those roles.

Most people, if only unconsciously, tend to perceive even the possibility of layoffs—much less the reality—as a threat to their livelihoods, their egos, their families, their careers, and more. The prospect of being rightsized or forced into a new role not of one's choosing, or having to develop new capabilities to stay relevant, or being shifted to a different part of the business with unknown bosses, colleagues, and expectations can all set off major hazard warnings in our minds.

Thus, restructuring represents a threat and triggers a Survive response, often a highly overheated Survive response, with significant feelings of fear, anxiety, and anger. Energy is directed at protecting oneself, if only unconsciously, and attention to the real business problems and opportunities can evaporate. Under these conditions, we have seen time and again that Survive overwhelms the Thrive Channel, and creativity (and any focus on handling a difficult situation faster, smarter, and more efficiently) ceases. Productivity and, more importantly, innovation drop—a potential disaster in volatile and uncertain times.

This is particularly harmful in the cases where the restructuring is precipitated by a new business model. The disruption that these innovations cause to internal operations, and the corresponding Survive Channel activation, lead to serious implementation challenges and in many cases can completely derail a transformation. Some people consider such implementation challenges inevitable. They are not. Consider Netflix shifting its business model from DVDs delivered in the mail to streaming content. For anyone involved with logistics or supply chain, the threats to their power, influence, and even jobs would have been very real. Yet Netflix drove the process in a way that avoided overheated Survive, and debilitating drops in productivity, creativity, and innovation did not happen.

Traditionally, firms muddle through common restructuring problems, some handling them better than others. In the past, as long as they managed the process minimally well, when they eventually established a new normal, stopped making internal changes, and stopped aggressive cost-cutting, people's anxiety, anger, and fear eventually did dissipate and individual productivity improved. But it can take a long time to regain trust in senior management, to start to feel safe again, to get over the loss of friends and survivor's guilt, and to start feeling more positive and passionate about future possibilities. *In a rapidly accelerating world, enterprises no longer have the luxury of that time*. Additionally, in a world of greater labor mobility, a poorly managed restructuring carries significant risks of talent retention.

The Growing Problem with the Traditional Method

To appreciate what works well today, it helps to clarify the traditional approach and understand why it increasingly fails to produce desired results.

Basically, restructuring has typically followed this path. Top management sets targets for cost savings, efficiencies, growth, profitability, or other performance measures in light of the state of the business. Consultants or insider experts analyze the organization of business activities and people. They match what they find to the desired operating model and look for redundancies. Top management makes the big decisions about activities, organizational structure, and timing (the latter referring to whether this should be executed in phases over years, in phases but relatively quickly, or in an immediate Big Bang). More often than not implementation is done by insiders, except where highly specialized expertise is needed. Detailed decisions can be made at the top, or more often by task forces or workstreams staffed with upper-middle managers. Then, at some point, corporate communication becomes heavily involved to work out how the decisions will be explained, and to whom, and when. Messages cascade down the hierarchy. HR and legal become involved to help with any layoffs. If there is a transformation office, they will play some project management role.

The problems with this traditional approach today include:

- As in the case of the typical strategic planning approach to change, with restructuring today often too much is happening too quickly. Small elite groups have neither the time nor the information to make the best decisions in any of the steps in the process.

- Even with good work from corporate communications, once the Survive Channel is activated, rumors and water cooler conversations can overwhelm messages from the top, both in volume and in believability. Trust in management easily goes down. Focus is diverted away from business problems and opportunities. The fact that restructurings so often seem to be only short-term cost-cutting exercises, no matter what corporate communications says, makes this all worse.

- Recovery of trust, attention, positive morale, and individual productivity comes far too slowly. In a 100-mph world, organizations are increasingly having to restructure more quickly and then immediately pivot into a growth, innovation mode. You don't have the luxury of time healing the wounds. In virtually all cases, any innovation and growth that a restructuring was supposed to help support does not materialize because of the lack of trust, the negative emotions, the narrow focus on threats and not on opportunities—all of which is directly related to an overheated Survive Channel and an underactivated Thrive Channel.

In general, the traditional approach was designed for a slower-moving and less complex world in which change happened less often, business cycles were longer, and innovation was less important.

Kraft Heinz: A Cautionary Tale

A dramatic example of today's basic restructuring problem began in 2015 and is still playing itself out, occasionally very visibly, as we write this today. The debacle makes headlines both because of the sheer magnitude of the problem and the fact that one of history's most outstanding business investors and leaders is a part of the story.

Kraft and Heinz (KHC) were put together in a $63 billion mega-merger initiated by the Brazilian investment firm 3G Capital and Warren Buffett's Berkshire Hathaway. When the merger was announced, much was said about strategic synergies and leveraging brands internationally. But if you examine what happened after the transaction was completed, you find an almost total focus on a particularly aggressive form of restructuring. The central vehicle (zero-based budgeting) helped management cut nearly $2 billion out of operating costs.

Best evidence suggests that the way KHC executed their post-merger restructuring did not just activate Survive, but triggered an overheated, overwrought Survive, and for a considerable amount of time. Employee data from Glassdoor, for example, shows a 15% drop in satisfaction scores following the merger, a dip that took two and a half years to improve. That is, for two and a half years, Thrive and the outcomes of Thrive (creativity and innovation to respond to changing consumer demands being key here) were being sucked out of the system. During this period, there is little to no evidence that staff who were closest to the marketplace were energetically looking for new opportunities, upbeat about the possibility of finding those opportunities, or innovating and collaborating to take advantage of those opportunities.

In the past, this might not have mattered much in a big firm with powerful brands and little threat of serious competition to those brands. A business would just suffer through this sort of restructuring. Eventually operations would bounce back after a winding down of the aggressive actions that were putting people into overheated Survive. But for a number of reasons, the marketplace for Kraft Heinz was not in its traditional state of little to slow change. Consumer tastes were increasingly shifting, with a concern for healthier food being a big trend. Competitors (old and, more so, new) were fulfilling those needs. Changes in the concentration of retailers were also putting significant price pressure on consumer goods companies. KHC struggled to keep share, much less grow it, and had to battle to maintain margins.

When it became clear that the restructuring was not on track, KHC senior management tried three ploys.

With growth not happening as expected, they kept cutting and laying off people in multiple rounds, to try to keep the profits and stock price up. This created even more overwrought Survive and lengthened the period of collapsed morale and lower individual productivity.

They also tried to do a merger using stock that had actually performed well after the short-term cost-cutting improvements from layoffs. The equity markets did not fully appreciate what was happening inside the firm. But the merger target, Unilever, seems to have been watching the 3G aggressive cost-cutting playbook and wanted no part of it (big surprise!). So Unilever fought against the merger and succeeded.

3G also did what is common in the PE world and increased the proportion of pay at KHC in the form of bonuses linked to performance metrics. At some point, no doubt partially motivated by these incentives, a few people in KHC's procurement department appear to have pushed the boundaries of what was legitimate, probably rationalizing that this was really okay or was just a short-term move to give the firm some breathing space. They were caught and "accounting irregularities" made the headlines.

What makes this story particularly important as an example of how a common approach to layoffs does not work in today's world is: (1) Buffett was involved, so it is impossible to write this off as mistakes made by a team of ill-informed or incompetent individuals. (2) The scale of the impact is vast. Over a few years, Buffett's stock holdings in KHC went down over $22 billion. Six years later, as we write this, the stock has yet to recover.

There is much evidence that, in general, restructuring has been growing. In a large study focused on layoffs, the researchers concluded that in 1979 fewer than 5% of Fortune 100 companies announced layoffs. A second study said that 45% of this group had layoffs 15 years later in 1994. And another study of 2,000 companies reported that 65% resorted to layoffs during and right after the 2008 recession.

This increase in the number of companies undergoing restructuring does not appear to have translated into more success. One credible study of "transformations" by Standard & Poor's and the Bruce Henderson Institute demonstrated that success rates have not been high. (Because of how they measured whether a transformation was going on, virtually all of them contained restructurings.) With a methodology that looked at actual numerical performance (not simply "opinion"), this study showed a failure percentage, defined as underperforming their industry benchmark in both one-year and five-year timeframes, of 70% in 2001 and 75% in 2012.

There is no reason we should expect restructurings will go down anytime soon. The opposite prediction better fits the data. The world needs a new approach that does not kill innovation and can help anyone roar out of a downturn, not limp.

A Method Compatible with Human Nature, the Modern Organization, and a Rapidly Changing Context

At the start of this chapter, you read an example that represents an alternative to the KHC story. It was an approach that avoids the problems associated with traditional restructuring and increases the probability of success. In it, leaders focus as much thought and energy on *how* changes are to be implemented as on determining *what* changes are necessary.

This process might be summarized as such:

- Build a case for change that highlights the future benefits of the restructuring.

- Engage employees and accelerate (real) results.
- Reinforce (and sustain) the momentum until the work is successful.

Build a Case for Change That Highlights the Future Benefits of the Restructuring

Too often, restructuring is framed as a burning platform, which reinforces and overactivates Survive. Hence the importance of pulling back and looking at bigger and longer-term opportunities.

To avoid this problem, it is important to build some sort of positive case for change in the hearts and minds of people. We do not mean hype, rah-rah, or unrealistic tripe. We mean a perspective, and the emotional tone that supports it, that puts the short-term reality in a broader, more realistic context of the biggest opportunities for the organization, its employees, its customers, and other relevant parties.

The drive to energize the Thrive Channel cannot be an exercise that ignores or downplays the short-term reality. It must produce an "opportunity statement" that is not only positive and compelling but is also honest about why the inherently disruptive restructuring is necessary. In the best examples we have been involved with, leaders pull no punches, but make it clear that the ultimate goal is much bigger and more inspirational than the immediate cost cutting or restructuring. In the case of the closure of five plants, this bigger goal was both the creation of a more sustainably competitive firm (with all the associated benefits) and a journey for those laid off that would actually lead to a comparable or better life situation than before.

The receptiveness of the organization to a Thrive-activating, forward-looking case for change is greatly increased by first calming Survive. Leaders can help by demonstrating a commitment to making the restructuring process minimally disruptive to employees and customers. Communication is essential, but as is so often the case with leadership, action consistent with words is even more important.

The specifics of communication have to fit the context; however, some common principles can guide the efforts.

First, be transparent and honest about why decisions are being made, the timelines, and most importantly the process being followed. Share the approach to severance packages, career placement services, and so on. Don't leave people guessing or let the rumor mill distort reality.

Second, demonstrate empathy. It is critical for top and mid-level leaders to seek to understand and have compassion for what employees are experiencing throughout the restructuring process. These conversations can be uncomfortable, and their own anxiety can lead managers to avoid or delay having such discussions. However, it is important for leaders to be visible and create two-way conversations that allow employees to ask questions.

Third, while it is generally too late to build trust in leadership during a restructuring, it is easy to damage the trust that already exists. By being consistent in what is said and what is done, as well as in how actions are taken, leaders can guard against the erosion of trust.

Top managers often underestimate how disruptive a restructuring can be. It is time well spent to ensure alignment among senior leaders, particularly the executive committee, not just on the case for change but also on how to minimize the anxiety and disruption felt by employees.

Engage Employees and Accelerate (Real) Results

Achieving positive change through restructuring requires a sustained sense of urgency and commitment among many people, not just a few top executives. From what we have seen, it is best to start where there is both energy *and* trust. The group charged with creating broad engagement must have credibility in the eyes of the employees. This group will generally need to include top management as well as a diverse team from all departments, levels, and geographic regions. The best groups include staff who are highly trusted, well-informed, influential, *and* who believe that positive outcomes are truly possible.

Engaging employees requires a vision that cannot be only of a smaller organization, a more cost-effective one, or a revamped structure. It has to be of a thriving enterprise that is able to achieve previously impossible outcomes. Or if a facility is shutting, the vision must include an acceptable or (ideally) a better future for laid-off employees.

The success of a restructuring effort is often determined by the specific initiatives, such as process improvements, new product designs, or new marketing strategies that accompany or enable the cost-reduction efforts. In selecting these initiatives, it is crucial to keep this in mind: *A central goal throughout the restructuring is to avoid inadvertently sending a firm into an overwrought Survive response, but instead to build credibility and momentum, to complete the restructuring faster rather than slower, and to pivot quickly into a post-restructuring, Thrive-oriented growth phase.*

The key during implementation is often the feelings induced—that the management of the firm really does care (or does not), has integrity (or does not), is trustworthy (or is not), wants to minimize disruption in lives (or is indifferent), is willing (or is not willing) to help people who have new demands placed on them, who have been reorganized, or who have been let go.

Successful implementation also requires empowering the employee base to act. Those closest to the work are often best suited to identify solutions, test hypotheses, fail-fast, and pivot when needed. When leaders focus on removing barriers and then getting out of the way, initiative teams and Thrive-energized volunteers can find creative solutions that make life better for the workforce, and ultimately for the business.

To quell skepticism, creating and celebrating short-term wins is essential. However, wins associated with a loss for some group should be treated with sensitivity—for example, growth in a new part of the business at the expense of an old part.

And while one would never celebrate successfully getting rid of 10% of the workforce, we can recognize the transparency of the process, celebrate individuals achieving their own objectives (like finding new jobs, deciding to retire, going back to school), and create enthusiasm for the changes that result in positive steps toward the opportunities that the restructuring makes possible (such as new investments, or gains in market share).

Reinforce (and Sustain) Until the Work is Successful

Even under ideal circumstances, after some human pain there may be calls to declare victory and stop, to denounce some decisions as unfair or inept or greedy, or just to give in to a collective sense of exhaustion. To sustain the gains, to continue the process with speed and efficiency, and to avoid any let-up that creates problems, more pain, overheated Survive, and the loss of needed Thrive, all the good work done at the beginning and middle of an effective restructuring needs to be carefully nurtured, reinforced, and sustained until the job is done. This observation may appear obvious to the point of seeming trivial. But remember that even our smartest methodologies are always working within a context of people and organizations that lean toward stability, survival, and threat avoidance, not change, opportunity, and a drive for continuous excellence. Let up because all seems well and the consequences can be very bad.

Outside of extreme cases like totally shutting down facilities, as in the first story in this chapter, success in this final phase usually requires focusing efforts on institutionalizing beneficial changes. For example, in many restructurings, critical training can be embedded in future development plans. Hiring and onboarding processes can be revisited to ensure they align to new structures and ways of working. Incentive plans and team structures can be redesigned to ensure consistent measurements are in place to help get ahead of the need for more restructuring down the line. And nothing sustains change like driving new norms and values into the very culture of the organization.

Current Reality versus What You Can Do

These two sets of restructuring processes—those that the best current research shows work well in a rapidly changing world versus the all-too-common current reality— are very different, obviously. The new is guided by analytics and feelings, not just analytics alone, with a focus on value and opportunity, not just short-term cost problems, and with many people driving change, not just a select few at or near the top of the hierarchy.

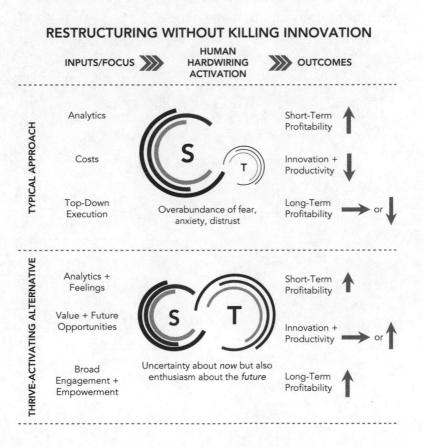

RESTRUCTURING WITHOUT KILLING INNOVATION

As a result, instead of creating an overabundance of anxiety, fear, and distrust, along with an overheated Survive and an under-activated Thrive, there is appropriately aroused Survive and Thrive. All of this leads to better outcomes for the combination of short-term profitability, innovation, and productivity, as well as long-term profitability.

The new approach has a sophistication based on neuroscience and human nature missing in the first, as well as a better appreciation of the change barriers inherent in the typical, modern organization. And it can produce results that will literally amaze many people.

Yes, amaze.

Chapter 6

Cultural Change That Helps You Adapt

A fourth way that enterprises try to cope with a more rapidly changing world is by attempting to consciously mold their "cultures" to be less an anchor holding back change and more a force that fosters speed and adaptability.

Unlike strategic planning, digital transformation, and restructuring, which tend to become highly quantified exercises, culture is generally treated as "soft." In a world where managerial processes dominate, and quantification has become more and more important and feasible, culture has been less often the center of intentional action for driving organizations into a prosperous future.

Nevertheless, culture lives on as an important issue because enough people intuitively believe statements like "Culture eats strategy for breakfast" (a comment often attributed to business guru Peter Drucker). That is, in terms of how powerful a force it is in driving action, culture might beat strategy by a lot. This same logic would probably lead to "Culture eats restructuring for a light afternoon snack."

In the last decade, the volume of conversation about culture and its impact on performance seems to have risen. A number of incredibly successful technology companies have talked of their cultures as a differentiator both for attracting talent and for operational performance. When high-flier Netflix codified and made available a description of its norms and values in a PowerPoint deck, the slides went viral. One tech superstar even called the presentation "the most important document to come out of the Valley."

So the promise of culture is widely recognized. And though it is common to read how this firm or that enterprise is changing its culture to propel growth, profitability, employee satisfaction, and the like, it is a struggle to find examples where these efforts have been demonstrably successful.

As with strategy, digital transformation, and restructuring, the problem is not that this methodology lacks possibilities. Quite the contrary: creating the right sort of culture has been shown to dramatically facilitate prospering within a complex and shifting context by helping execute a sound strategy or by helping with adaptation in general.

The problem here, again, is rooted in human nature, the modern organization, common leading change mistakes, and an inadequate understanding of all three. It is also exacerbated in this case by fuzziness about exactly what culture is, where it comes from, and thus how to change it. The latter is most centrally an exercise in action, not messaging, which produces vision-relevant results. We call them "wins" that are an improvement over the "old ways."

What Is "Culture"?

Just as one can reasonably say that strategy came from the military and didn't really land solidly in business or other organizations until the 1970s, culture came from the social anthropological study of remote societies and, with a few exceptions, did not really land in business and related worlds until the 1980s.

Social anthropology was born in academia during the late nineteenth and early twentieth centuries when the availability of research funding, new long-distance transportation options, and interest in societies different from mainline industrializing nations all converged. People like Margaret Mead, Ann Benedict, and Bronislaw Malinowski traveled to and lived in villages in the South Seas, or in Native American reservations. First, they simply described what life was like at their sites, then tried to understand why that life was in so many ways decisively different from what they were used to. In the process, they locked onto the concept of "culture," which tended to be defined very broadly. As they used the term, it represented virtually anything in a group that was passed on from one generation to the next, including how one should behave, the technologies and tools one used, the clothes one wore, the foods one ate, the rites and rituals which were observed, and so on.

Four of the more important conclusions early scholars drew are all still highly relevant today.

First, people often have great difficulty describing their own cultures, or agreeing on what their cultures are. Second, people have difficulty at least in part because cultural attributes were passed down informally and not through any intentional process. Newcomers and children are praised when they behave in culturally appropriate ways and sanctioned or ridiculed when they do not—often quite unconsciously and with no formally coordinated action. Third, though essentially invisible, culture is nevertheless a very powerful force. People sometimes make huge sacrifices, or even die, to remain true to cultural norms and values. And fourth, cultures tend to be remarkably stable and to change very slowly.

The concept of organizational culture took off in business due partially to a best selling book by Harvard's Terrence Deal and Allan Kennedy in 1982. But even more fundamentally, it came through interest in Japanese consumer electronics and automotive enterprises (like Sony, Panasonic, Toyota, and Nissan), which were expanding beyond Japan and beating domestic competition impressively. Studies of this phenomenon pointed to cultures inside Japanese firms that were "strong" and that seemed to value—much more than a typical American business did—both the quality of products, as seen from a customer perspective, and employee loyalty. These cultures also seemed less obsessed with short-term financial results, particularly within top management. In some quarters, the cry went out that U.S. business needed to learn from the Japanese.

Throughout the increasingly changing 1980s and 1990s, growing numbers of enterprises talked about developing their cultures into a source of competitive advantage.

Within the business world, if there was a reigning theory about the relationship of culture to results, it was that "strong cultures" were winners. In a strong culture, everyone automatically seemed to work out of the same playbook. Hence great teamwork was created, as seen in Japanese enterprises. And without a boss having to instruct and constantly monitor activity to create that teamwork, organizations could both move more quickly and use fewer hierarchical resources.

Corporate Culture and Performance

Aware of this growing interest in corporate culture, in 1979 one of us (Kotter) began a series of studies with a colleague at Harvard Business School, Professor James Heskett. Our guiding questions were: Is there a relationship between internal firm culture and its economic performance over a decade or so? If yes, what was that relationship? Were "strong" cultures associated with better performance? If not, did any sort of culture seem to help drive better results? And if yes, then how do you change a culture to make it a driver of high performance?

We ended up doing four studies. One involved around two hundred medium and large companies. Two studies included a carefully selected group of matched sets (a total of 12 "winners" and 10 "laggards" in ten industries). The final inquiry focused on eleven case studies of firms successfully changing their cultures to help them win in their respective industries. This work was both quantitative and qualitative. And it involved finding and enlisting expert observers, convincing firms to allow us to do interviews, and traveling to work face-to-face on site.

All this was reported in detail in a book entitled *Corporate Culture and Performance*. For our purposes here, the most interesting findings are as follows.

First, there was some relationship—but not much—between "strong" cultures and three measures of decade-long financial results. Strong cultures were extremely influential, but we found it was quite possible for a firm to have what might be called a strong but toxic culture, where norms driving behavior and shared values were powerful but not the slightest bit competitively helpful. At that time, General Motors may have been the poster child for this kind of situation. At GM, a powerful culture had developed up and down the hierarchy after years and years of dominance in its industry. But that culture supported norms of behavior such as not listening to or watching non-Detroit competitors closely, acting with arrogance, and not valuing much innovation relevant to customers or stockholders.

Second, we found that cultures that were compatible with business strategies were often associated with superior financial performance. The causality appeared to be simple. Such cultures made it much easier to implement the strategies well and quickly. If the strategy was a smart adaptation to a changing business environment, then the new culture accelerated that jump into the future.

But the association to performance was still weak in this second case for a number of reasons. Strategies could be bad, and more efficiently executing a bad strategy obviously did not create great results. Also, the world could change, demanding a new strategy that was not compatible with the culture, which tended to change slowly if at all. And shifts in the external environment or the stage of a company's maturity could render a once appropriate culture no longer helpful.

Some people consider Uber a very visible recent case of one of these problems. The firm's culture of ultra-competitive meritocracy and hustle may have initially helped it to expand rapidly, ahead of potential rivals, while regulatory authorities were still catching up to the new travel innovation. But that same set of norms and values may have become a drag on performance once regulatory authorities started to question its business practices. Certainly, the built-in tendency to push the edges of what's legal and the drive to win at all costs, combined with elements that were never helpful, like harassment and bullying, no doubt empowered authorities to limit or restrict Uber's access to various markets.

Third, we found cultures that seemed to be relatively rare but were clearly connected to superior performance. At their core, they highly valued the interests of all the enterprises' major constituencies, particularly customers, stockholders, and employees, and thus managers and executives paid close attention to these factors. They also upheld the norm that people up and down the hierarchy were expected to help initiate action when changes of any sort created new and unsatisfied needs within these constituencies.

Causality seemed to operate this way. The world changes. Because of cultural norms, the multi-stakeholder view, and the expectation to act, many eyeballs are looking for relevant changes in product or service markets, labor markets, financial markets, relevant communities, and legislation. No matter where they are in the hierarchy, when people see relevant stakeholder change they are inclined to try to initiate responses to adapt. Thus we called these winning cultures "adaptive." Where the core norms and values are strong enough, we found that adaptation could even lead to changing more peripheral or less central elements of the culture itself. So once such a culture was in place, it helps an organization adapt to more rapid and complex change, even to some degree by changing itself.

Fourth, we discovered that most attempts to change cultures in any significant way to fit new demands or to be adaptive in general were not very successful. It was unclear from the limited case studies we did why this was so, or why a few firms did succeed. But one pattern seemed clear. The head of the organization was very important. If he or she made cultural change a personal crusade, it had a much higher chance of succeeding. If he or she treated it as one of numerous initiatives, or delegated it pretty much entirely to human resources, success was elusive.

Changing Culture

Over the last decade, we have learned much more about cultural change as a means of helping organizations deal with a more volatile and rapidly moving world. The finding about the importance of the most senior person in an organization is still very much a valid observation. But much more is involved. And the overall pattern is not at all inconsistent with what we have been describing in the case of strategy, digital transformation, and restructuring.

The core of the successful culture change pattern seems to be this. Somehow, perhaps deliberately or perhaps randomly, a group of people alter how they *act*, typically because they see an opportunity for something better (i.e. their Thrive Channel is sufficiently activated). Thus new actions are found that are not naturally driven by, or even consistent with, the existing culture. At first, because these actions challenge the status quo, they may activate a Survive response in others. But in successful cultural change, this initiative succeeds at producing what people perceive as better results. These results could be financial, or the achievement of virtually anything that has been committed to as a goal or opportunity. These "wins" are recognized, communicated, and celebrated. The recognition, communication, and celebration activate Thrive for more people, and encourage additional smart and needed action that is counter-cultural. That, in turn, produces still more wins. After a while, with momentum building, a growing number of people start to develop what might best be called new mindsets. As long as something does not shut down this enlarging dynamic of more new actions, more perceived success linked to the actions, more recognition/communication/celebration, and more new mindsets, then new habits start to form. Eventually, individual habits become group habits, or essentially something new/changed in the culture.

At first, a new or changed culture is still fragile. But if the behavioral norms and shared values are reinforced by new employee training, compensation and other rewards, top management behavior, and so on, the culture will solidify—at which point one can accurately say it has changed.

If one is trying to create a culture that not only fits a strategy or external market conditions but is also adaptive to whatever comes next, the new actions and perceived wins must address the real needs or expectations of all key constituencies: customers, employees, and owners. And these actions need to come from all levels in the hierarchy. In this way, the iterative process eventually creates the sort of culture that research shows helps adaptation of any sort.

CHANGING CULTURE

In Chapter 2 we described how the Survive/Thrive system developed through human evolution over many thousands of years. The formation and evolution of human and organizational cultures is in some ways similar. The random mutation that starts the sequence of change in our hardwiring is replaced in firms with either a deliberate or an accidental change in behaviors. But in both cases, when the mutation or action creates an advantage, a process begins that in turn can lead to new human hardwiring or corporate culture.

Because of all the looping, momentum building, and steps in the process, the sustained cultural change described above really does require time. One often hears in the business press a report of how "in the past year we have successfully changed the culture," which, unless we are talking about a very small organization, is a fantasy. At best, in such cases something useful has changed that eventually could alter the culture. Such changes could include a few potentially important behaviors, or mindsets, or individual habits for some people—but not organizational culture.

In the final study in the *Corporate Culture and Performance* research, we found in 11 cases of major cultural change, it took the generally sizable firms 4–10 years back then to make this happen. They started seeing better results in the first year and some very impressive results in the second year. But in terms of a new culture that fit a new strategy, which in turn fit changed external conditions, or better yet a new adaptive culture, considerable time was required.

What is needed to get this cultural change process moving and sustain it until there is real change for the better? The best evidence says *a lot*. Why? Again, we come back first to human nature and the modern organization. The former easily perceives new actions as a threat to one's comfortable relationship with a boss, status with peers, ability to meet job objectives—the list is long—and Survive Channels send us into fight-or-flight mode to shut change down. The latter, the modern organization, is designed for smooth operations, stability, reliability, and efficiency, all of which resist nontrivial new behavior. And in the case of culture, unless its core is "adaptive" (i.e. stakeholder focus looking for changes and empowerment up and down the hierarchy allowing people to act on what they see), it too can be a natural and powerful source of stability.

What then can overcome these forces? Here again we come back to themes that should at this point in the book start to sound familiar. A diverse and growing many, not just a select few taking new action. People acting in new ways because their hearts, not just their minds, are directing them to want to, not just to have to. Proactive action not just directed from the top via operating plans and budgets and hierarchy. Instead, movement because people in the middle and on the front lines actually help provide some leadership for cultural change. More often than not, momentum is started because a powerful enough group sees not just changes happening around them but the opportunities that change provides. And they develop, first for themselves and then in more and more colleagues, a true sense of urgency to do something to take advantage of those opportunities.

In the case of culture, and to some degree for most of the methods addressed in this book, one more tactic can help greatly. Because of the time required to change culture, people need to see that progress is not only possible but is happening. Therefore, it is essential to be on the lookout for leading indicators, those metrics that should logically shift as a part of a journey toward cultural change.

So, first, is any new behavior happening that is reflective of your vision of the norms and values you want to develop (because they fit your new strategy or fit new external realities)? Initially, if the answer is yes (because, for example, cross-functional email traffic is up in an organization trying to grow faster because of a more collaborative culture), even if there are no new and better business results (no growth in revenues, new customers, better margins), the behavior itself can be a very important leading indicator of success in your change effort. Later, are we beginning to see this action producing some business- or mission-relevant wins? Not a whole new culture, just some wins (revenue growth, number of customers, profitability growth, etc.)? Then, still later, are these wins being celebrated and communicated sufficiently, and do you have measures that take you beyond anecdotes? Then, are the new actions consistent with the desired culture growing? And so on: some new mindsets, some new habits?

Leading indicators are logical to know and keep track of in any significant change effort. They seem to be essential in keeping Thrive activated over long periods. Yet they are ignored all the time.

We have seen any number of cases where enterprises were successfully molding culture in a way to make the firms more adaptive to faster change. Yet with stock price going down, or revenues flat, or some other key metrics refusing to move, people abandoned their effective efforts since the data seemed to suggest they were failing. We have no idea how often this happens, but it is clear it is not uncommon—and a very tragic mistake.

What Leads to Failed Culture Change?

Anecdotally we hear that interest is growing in using culture as an adaptive mechanism to drive change internally to take advantage of a more rapidly shifting world. It is difficult to measure with any degree of certainty how much this interest is converting into success. But it is easy to find and document efforts that are only partial successes or outright failures.

There are pretty clear patterns associated with the failures. A typical example is a large international electronics firm that announced a few years ago that it was changing its culture to make the firm faster moving, more responsive to shifts in customer demands, and more innovative. A hand-picked group of a dozen executives, many from HR, had a series of meetings and did some top-level interviews to clarify what culture they believed was needed. Their conclusions were written down and summarized as eight points about values or behavior. The output from these meetings went to the executive committee for their approval. With minor tweaks, approval was given.

Then the statement of culture was given to two small teams, one in corporate communications and the other in HR. These groups drew up plans for "cascading" the information down the hierarchy and "educating" management about the new culture. Ultimately, the message was not that this was the culture the firm aspired to, much less anything about how the enterprise was going to create the new culture. The message was: *This is our culture*.

When the communication and subsequent education sessions produced little to no change, they were supplemented by speeches at management meetings and a few open "townhalls." Another HR team was ordered to put together a two-hour education module to be included in new employee orientation sessions.

Four years later, in January 2020, based on survey results from 1,350 people, the website comparably.com gave the firm a culture score of less than 3.5 on a 5.0 scale, putting it in the bottom 30% of firms that had been rated.

The problems with this typical approach are multifold. It is too light and quick a touch, given all the barriers to cultural change thrown up by human nature, modern organizations, and the very stable essence of culture itself. This approach focuses on telling and not on showing, on talk and not on action, which will never sustain an activated Thrive. It is essentially a management solution to what is in fact more of a leadership problem. When people think, "No, this is not our culture," that can evoke cynicism, which lessens trust in management, which in turn can start to activate Survive. It is even possible that if an overactivated Survive state goes on long enough, this will not only exhaust people but will lead to behavior that can change culture in ways that do not lead to organizational prosperity. A norm develops, for example, not to act on any communication cascaded from the top, unless it is trivial or highly verifiable.

Yet despite all these problems, this methodology persists today, not least because it fits easily with the mindset built into the modern organization, which leans toward top-down communication and execution, elite groups, and silos that own specific areas (culture goes to HR).

Changing an Entrenched Culture to Get Far Better Results

The pharmaceutical industry is heavily regulated and places great emphasis on quality to protect the public. A divisional CEO in one well-known company came to realize that its quality culture had evolved to be one of "checking-the-boxes" rather than a mindset of doing the right thing and constantly improving.

The compliance culture manifested in a shop floor workforce that was entirely focused on following the rules and not at all on innovating to improve productivity or, for example, suggesting better ways of lowering rejected batches of product and waste—even though some floor employees had ideas for how to do so. That, in turn, meant the company was both struggling to keep up with customer orders and receiving increasing warnings from regulatory agencies.

As described by the Chief Quality Officer, "Our first task was to make the leaders appreciate the seriousness of the situation (which included a likely warning letter from the FDA) and that it would not be solved by the same old approaches." Recognizing a need to make not only an intellectual appeal but an emotional one as well, he used an old internet video about human suffering when enough of their quality product was not available because of manufacturing difficulties. The leadership team discussed how they felt about the situation and whether their current/traditional approach would get them out of the crisis. By having the group come to a conclusion on their own that a change was necessary, instead of pushing a problem and a solution at them with PowerPoint logic, the Chief Quality Officer believes he avoided generating Survive-driven resistance.

After much discussion, the leadership concluded that improving quality required changing the culture and that could not be achieved through a traditional project or initiative. The key, they decided, was engaging the shop floor employees in a new way and breaking down the barriers between management and the shop floor. In essence, they wanted to create an environment for more Thrive activation, creating more openness, innovation, and a willingness to experiment with new and potentially better ways of working. Culture would change, they came to believe, when new actions and behaviors were demonstrated and rewarded.

The importance of engaging employees in this change resulted in the creation of a new role: Head of Innovation and Engagement for Quality. The individual in this role, along with an initial group of engaged employees, recruited volunteers from all levels of the organization. By utilizing technology, they began to create a community and a movement. New ideas were developed, starting with a few vocal supporters on the shop floor. These improvement ideas were rapidly piloted, implemented, and celebrated. By leveraging technology and a peer-to-peer communication strategy, the early contributions were recognized and widely communicated. This encouraged others to participate in suggesting changes and improvements, building positive energy. As one employee noted, "This was the first time in my 15 years of working here that I felt valued for my ideas."

Momentum built as these "wins" continued to be celebrated in creative new ways. As an example, one region created a "Win of the Week (WOW)" award, where shop floor employees got to present their idea to the top leadership. The visibility of the successes and the support from leadership encouraged more and more employees to exhibit these new behaviors, resulting in an emerging culture that felt entirely different.

Unlike some past attempts at "culture change" in this organization, this time the leaders did not tell people what culture they wanted. Instead, they were able to demonstrate the behaviors and actions that would result from this culture. "In a steady state, how we act and behave is heavily influenced by culture, but changing culture starts from changing the behaviors, not the other way around," said the Chief Quality Officer.

The impact of the cultural change was visible not just in new and more useful behaviors but in measurable performance and quality indices. Among other metrics, the firm saw a 25% reduction in human errors and sterility failures. Accidents and high-risk "events" fell by 50%. Write-off costs dropped dramatically, saving the company 250–350 million euros.

One key professional from the FDA, after helping write a blisteringly negative review of one of this firm's plants, came back two years later and told the Chief Quality Officer that he was "shocked." "What I see today," he said, "is so different from what I saw not that long ago that I am truly amazed. The quality numbers have shifted more and faster than I have ever seen. But even more so, the attitudes and actions of the management and staff have shifted—in some cases, quite radically." The shift was so dramatic that the FDA representative asked how they might replicate this success within the entire industry.

Business Culture Writ Large

We have been focusing in this chapter on the culture of individual organizations. There are other, broader cultures. Perhaps the broadest and most well-known are national cultures. Indeed, even today when the word "culture" is in the vernacular, it is more likely to refer to France versus Japan than Apple versus Google, much less Kellogg versus General Mills.

There is also something that might best be called business culture. This goes far beyond single organizations or, in some cases, even nations. You can deduce it by reading the most influential parts of the business press or finding what messages are explicitly or implicitly sent out in business education. Both national and business cultures in turn are relevant to our discussion here because they do influence firm-level norms and values—sometimes for the good, sometimes not.

One element of business culture that has been making it even more challenging for many firms to keep ahead in a faster-moving world is the powerful belief that the purpose of a business is to "maximize shareholder gain." This has been translated into norms about quarterly reporting of financial results that put CEOs under great pressure to pay close attention to a narrow set of short-term financial metrics. This same business culture has been pushing top executives to take actions to meet projected quarterly financial targets, especially earnings per share, even if they don't think those actions are best for most shareholders, much less for customers and employees, or for dealing with longer-term business issues.

Driven by the broader business culture, this resulting firm-level culture has, in two ways, become more of an obstacle than an asset in a rapidly moving world. First, focusing so much on the short-term makes it more difficult in general for any enterprise trying to actually change its culture, to make it more of an adaptive force or at least a strategy-implementation asset, because cultural change of any magnitude takes time. Second, by focusing top management's eyes on stockholders, firms all too often do not have enough people paying enough attention to and then acting swiftly on changes in the product/service marketplace, in labor markets, among important suppliers, or in the key communities in which they have a significant presence.

The mindset that the role of business is solely to maximize profits and hence stock valuation has in general made business leaders hesitant to engage on issues that don't seemingly impact their business directly. With the growing activist nature of both employees and customers, this is becoming an increasingly untenable position. Leaders are coming under pressure from their employees and customers to take public positions and actions on topics from environmental sustainability, to racial and economic equity, to the choice of partnerships, to the broad issue of diversity, equity, and inclusion in the workplace.

The Business Roundtable (BRT), a lobbying group made up of the CEOs of the 200 largest businesses in the U.S., put out a statement in August 2019 saying that this must change. They said that in studying what they too had been promoting, they had concluded the "maximize shareholder return" perspective was no longer a sensible purpose for businesses. They instead wrote something that reads very much like our findings in the *Corporate Culture and Performance* studies. Most people today call this a "multi-stakeholder" view of purpose.

Immediately after publishing this declaration, which was accompanied by nearly all 200 signatures from the

CEO membership, it was praised, questioned, and attacked in article after article, blog after blog for months (until COVID-19 and its economic fallout completely overtook business news).

Those attacking the BRT proposal frequently argued that trying to serve many constituencies would lead to many metrics, no clear priorities, a loss of focus, and the poor overall results associated with lack of focus. There is some logic to this point, yet the most economically successful firms in the *Corporate Culture and Performance* studies nevertheless all somehow avoided this problem. Other critics employed economic theory and Adam Smith, saying the evidence has always been there that modern capitalism works best when people have a crystal-clear focus on profits alone. Implicit in the latter articles and blogs was the assertion that business culture had been focused on maximizing shareholder gain for centuries. Which is, in fact, not true.

If one goes back to the 1970s, before the latest round of accelerating change took off, virtually no one talked about the shareholder paradigm. It was not in the business press. It was not taught in business schools (one of us saw this firsthand at Harvard Business School at the time). More generally, it was not a part of the overall business culture. But during the 1970s and 1980s, that all changed, for a number of reasons.

The competitive landscape heated up, as businesses in Europe and Japan, decimated by WWII, came on strong internationally. Suddenly, growing profits did not come so easily for well-known U.S. enterprises. Also, savings and pension funds were being handled by a new breed of institutional investor, who felt the heat of a poor stock market in the 1970s, and passed on that pressure to firms in which they had large holdings. At the same time, a whole school of economic thought began loudly to champion the shareholder mantra. Then compensation for CEOs and other top management became tied much more to stock price.

And all this seemed to work. The stock market throughout most of the 1980s and 1990s did much better by some indices. And so the shareholder-first-and-foremost attitude became a part of the broader business culture.

But today we have nearly 50 years of evidence that shows some of the negative consequences of a share-holder maximization paradigm in a time of increasingly rapid change. We also have evidence that this paradigm did not even increase average stock market returns except briefly in the earliest days of its use. We now have a growing number of CEOs (although it is unclear how many) who seem to be trying to guide their firms in the general direction of the new BRT proclamation.

Will sufficient numbers of the Business Roundtable CEOs take action beyond just words, get some better results, communicate and celebrate the results, take more actions, and eventually shift staff mindsets into a better direction, then some habits, and then eventually their own individual cultures and their collective business culture? We will see.

We all have a stake in what happens next. It is hard to make an argument that no cultural change is the right solution for the vast majority of individual businesses or for business culture in general in an era of rapid, complex volatility. We need many more cultures that can facilitate prosperity in an era of speed and uncertainty. We need many more organizations that understand the science of culture change.

We think it is pretty clear what smart firms will do. What we need is for them to do it sooner rather than later and, in the process, help drive a broader shift in business culture that could benefit many, many people.

Chapter 7

Mergers and Acquisitions That Create Real Value

A fifth way that enterprises today try to deal with a more rapidly changing and often perplexing world is through the acquisition of a solution to some perceived change challenge. Instead of creating something new (a product, a marketing approach, a technology, etc.) via a revised strategy, trying to jump into the digital future in a big way, restructuring, or cultural renewal, they purchase or merge with an entity that already has what they think they need to better compete or better fulfill their mission.

As the rate of change has accelerated over the past three decades in a more complicated world, so has M&A activity, as we would logically expect. A good estimate is that the value of deals during this period has grown four-fold.

Often, M&A is driven by a simple economic evaluation. In light of our assessment of the way the world is moving, we conclude we need X: a revenue boost, less expense and higher margins, a particular technology or product or market, certain talent, and so on. Building that reality through internal changes alone will likely cost such and such, and that could be even higher because of internal disputes, uncertainties, lack of expertise in some new areas, and bureaucracy. We can buy the capability for less, guaranteed. So we buy.

Even more often these days, time is the issue. Sooner or later we can change ourselves so that we will have a capability or cost structure or better patents than our competition has. But that could take two years, four, or even longer. With M&A, we can achieve what is needed to help us survive and prosper in one-half or one-fourth the time. And in a rapidly moving competitive context, time is a big issue.

This way of responding to change leans heavily on all four approaches described in the previous chapters. That is, M&A is often followed by a new strategy, involves some restructuring and digital transformation, and always requires cultural integration. And more than any other reason, those integration problems lead to the M&A track record we see today.

The M&A Track Record Today

Mergers and acquisitions are a big business for investment banking, some law firms, some consulting firms, and most big accounting firms. The investment banks search for deals and help firms structure transactions and set prices. Consultants do analysis of possible transactions, especially from a competitive strategy point of view. The lawyers handle the contracts. The big accounting firms guide the "integration" of separate hierarchies, systems/policies, and nowadays especially complex IT infrastructures.

Reading business publications gives one the impression that many significant deals around the world happen every day. For the most part, the news is that these deals do well. Smaller M&A activity is harder to keep track of, but it is undoubtedly even more numerous. Occasionally, deals fall apart before the transaction is completed. And occasionally transactions go through but are then universally judged to be failures in two, four, or six years. Yet the common view is that, overall, M&A is done competently enough, and produces good enough results—which is why it is so prevalent. Just look at some of the most well-known big tech companies. They might do more than 100 acquisitions a year. And they are stars.

Researchers who have looked at value creation through M&A usually draw more critical conclusions. A variety of failure percentages have been reported, but virtually all are far more common than "occasionally." It is not unusual to find researchers arguing that more than half of M&A transactions do not gain the "synergies" that justified the deals in the first place. These non-success percentages range from 50 to 70% (not unlike some figures thrown around for strategy failures or restructuring disappointments). One thoughtful study reported in *Harvard Business Review* in 2011 put the failure rate even higher, somewhere between 70 and 90%.

In retrospect, sometimes the problem was incredibly myopic deals. The "smartest folks in the room" come out looking not so smart. Or the inability to innovate (i.e. change) in a shifting marketplace virtually forces top teams into trying deals they know are far less than perfect but produce short-term revenue growth that might make financial markets happy.

Yet the most obvious failures we have found seem to be at the integration stage. They come in two forms.

In the first, the focus is driven by a checklist of integration tasks and a process that has many similarities with typical strategy and restructuring work today. That is, the process is driven by a small group, at least some of whose hearts are not entirely in it, communicating little about the opportunities now available to the organization and its people. Managerial mindsets, metrics, and analytics dominate. To speed up what can take a long time, and to keep people from "worrying" or organizing to fight decisions, little is communicated about what employees should expect in terms of timelines, implications for various roles, and the like. Of course, all this inadvertently overheats Survive in too many people.

Virtually every item on a typical integration checklist can be picked up by our Survive Channel as a threat. New organization structure: your job could be missing. New set of marketing policies: what you have worked with successfully for a decade could be shifted or eliminated, making it impossible for a while at least to do your job at your expected standard. New budget and budgeting process: key projects could be cut and tacit knowledge of how to play the budgeting game may be no longer valid. New IT system: the potential horrors are unspeakable.

With standard modern organizational processes, and with too many people in an overheated Survive mode, the best data is never brought to bear in making crucial decisions. Too many employees are worrying about themselves and not about creating a great, new, integrated entity. Work happens too slowly (overheating

Survive even more). Or key people are forced to move quickly without needed data or time to make sensible decisions.

The second integration problem, and what we have seen as possibly an even deadlier one, is cultural.

THE CHALLENGE WITH M&A INTEGRATION

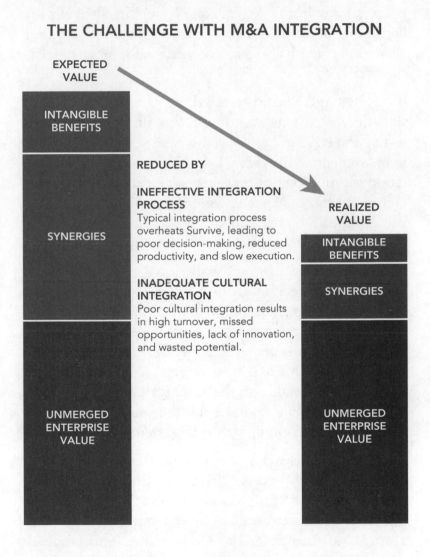

EXPECTED VALUE

INTANGIBLE BENEFITS

SYNERGIES

UNMERGED ENTERPRISE VALUE

REDUCED BY

INEFFECTIVE INTEGRATION PROCESS
Typical integration process overheats Survive, leading to poor decision-making, reduced productivity, and slow execution.

INADEQUATE CULTURAL INTEGRATION
Poor cultural integration results in high turnover, missed opportunities, lack of innovation, and wasted potential.

REALIZED VALUE

INTANGIBLE BENEFITS

SYNERGIES

UNMERGED ENTERPRISE VALUE

M&A Integration: The Usual Mistakes

A midsize West Coast tech company was presented with an acquisition idea by an advisory firm. The target enterprise was 15 years old and had a number of interesting patents in fields directly related to the growth plans of the potential acquirer. The relatively young firm had already had some success in a market that the potential acquirer wanted to enter. It also had a reputation for talented technical staff.

The target's board rejected the first offer as too low. But after discussions with the PE firm that had the largest ownership stake in the desired business, and after a 35% improvement of the offer, a deal was made. The expectation was that even at that price some revenue enhancements and cost efficiencies would rather quickly lead to a market valuation greater than the combined valuations of the individual firms.

As soon as the transaction closed, a large consulting firm that offers integration services swept in and ran everyone through their process of integration. The consultants helped create and staff a new combined hierarchy. Some people at the acquired entity were let go, and a few voluntarily left. More than two dozen consultant system integrators descended on the firm, taking over a number of offices where they worked full time stitching together a minimally functioning single IT system.

Other efficiencies came from consolidation of offices. A brief process, driven by the buying firm, defined the new entity's strategy and "values." Initial branding decisions were made and implemented. The process was disruptive, and likely missed opportunities as it was driven by people not close to the work. But removing obvious duplication in costs and taking advantage of the larger firm's supply chain and customer access provided enough early momentum that the initial grade given to the acquisition was a satisfactory one.

Signs of culture clash came early but were treated as business-as-usual under the circumstances. It was not as if the two firms had such radically different cultures that integration had been considered to be problematic. But they were at different stages of maturity, with the predictable differences that tend to follow.

The acquirer had more formal policies and processes that many in the newly acquired firm saw as "bureaucracy" in the negative sense. As the buyer, the bigger and older firm also ran the integration show, which felt "bossy" to those within their new acquisition. The latter had maneuvered with a considerable degree of autonomy from the very beginning and had maintained a sense of being in charge for 15 years, mostly through good performance relative to owner expectations. So there was water cooler grumbling in the younger firm about the heavy-handed bureaucrat, which was interpreted by the older firm as a resistance to establishing needed reliability and accountability. Viewed from the experiences of the older firm, the employees in their acquisition were operating without sufficient discipline.

Then during the first yearly planning cycle, more and more disagreements erupted about goals, strategies, methods, even the planning process itself. If it were not immediately obvious that most people on one side of the debates were from the older firm and most on the other were from the acquisition, that became clear soon enough. Partially to avoid conflict, people tended to retreat to interacting with their former colleagues in traditional ways, leaving out the "other" group.

At first, the corporate CEO was patient and truly listened. But the clock was ticking, and most of what he saw seemed to fit into the view that the younger firm was still trying (inappropriately) to operate as if it was a small startup. So he became more heavy-handed, pointing out, accurately, that they did not have the luxury of debating for another six months.

Reactions among many managers and technical staff who had come in through the acquisition grew increasingly dark. Many started to say that they should never have allowed themselves to be sold and that their very special culture was being lost or destroyed. None of these people could entirely explain how the older firm had been doing as well as it had, and the explanations they developed were generally not flattering.

Anxiety and anger began to grow on both sides. Turnover increased, some of which was forced. Those from the acquisition who stayed often fell into a pattern of passive resistance. In an industry that demands daily innovation, creativity slowed and in some cases died. Overheated Survive was killing Thrive.

With all the talent, technology, brands, and market penetration, a dysfunctional organization was still able to amble along. But the aspirations that led to the acquisition were largely unmet. What the marketplace might have seen as really cool innovative products never appeared. The stock did okay, but billions more that investors initially hoped for, including some large pension plans, did not materialize. After winning a few "great place to work" awards during its independent years, the acquisition became another okay workplace, with more typical stresses and strains on individuals and families.

Overall, hardly a disaster. But what a waste.

And it is far from unique. Think of high-profile cases like Daimler and Chrysler, Nextel and Sprint, or on a smaller scale Nest and Dropcam.

The Integration Problem and Solution

More than ever before, the M&A integration problem today is related to human nature. Specifically, M&A work is commonly done in ways from beginning to end that overactivate the Survive Channel in people's brains, dampen Thrive, and undermine the change needed to realize the deal's potential value.

The threat of a possible job loss, the uncertainty associated with what job you might be offered, the question of whether a new boss or boss's boss will appreciate your value, the worry that informal understandings about the next stages in your career may no longer be valid, and much more can overheat Survive and deactivate Thrive. Thus, integration can drag out and risk the very problem more and more enterprises face with restructuring in general: while you go into an innovation black hole, some of the competition adapts to marketplace needs and desires and takes away share and/or gains in momentum that can be hard for you to regain.

Even in large mergers, some of the big consulting firms move remarkably quickly through the process of integrating structures, systems, jobs, policies, and other core managerial elements found in all modern organizations. This is typically done in closed rooms with little to no involvement from employees, leading not just to anxiety but also to missed opportunities. In most cases, the consulting firms are not asked to finish the job and make sure there is one coherent and sensible culture. The new firm may take on that job by itself. If so, it usually does the work in the way that is the norm today. And that does not bode well.

Or the new firm basically ignores cultural integration altogether and runs into all the predictable problems that creates. Even when the integration consultants are asked to deal with culture, more often than not they approach the task in ways that make the typical mistakes we outlined in the previous chapter on culture. So you hit a wall of competing cultures that slows down decision-making and execution, and, far from combining the talent of both organizations, leads to turnover and loss of capabilities.

Research shows the solution is to recognize the potential cultural integration problem before the deal is signed. Add that factor into any risk analysis—which means you might back out of some projects. If the risk seems economically acceptable, start planning for the cultural integration immediately and launch it on day one alongside other integration activities. There will be cases where you may actually start with the cultural integration.

The method that works best was described in the last chapter. The core is all about new actions, better outcomes, achievements recognized and communicated and celebrated, more action, more results, recognition, communication, and celebration—all framed within the context of the biggest opportunities in front of the newly merged organization, often within the context of the question "What is possible today that was not possible yesterday?" Then comes some new mindsets among people in both the former organizations, mindsets that are similar and helpful in dealing with a rapidly changing world. Then with more momentum come new habits, again among some people from both the buyer and seller or the two merged parties. Then with time comes a new, single, sensible culture.

In the most successful cases in which we have been involved, because time is always an issue, all this is done with some strategic view as to where inside the new firm cultural integration is more or less important. Then the focus from day one is on the crucial, more important pieces, to move them along faster. Less important pieces take lower priority.

In one recent merger that created the largest firm in its business in the world, top management decided that problems in the integration of the two sales forces could be especially costly. If the two sales forces failed to integrate quickly and well, the CEO felt the entire merger was at risk. He knew from past experience that the combined sales group needed not only to implement new systems and policies, remove redundancies, and fast track training, but it also needed to build a strong culture of high-quality teamwork. He and the head of the new salesforce also judged that such a culture could not be easily created, at least not in a timely manner, since the two sales teams had been battling each other as enemy number one for years. So they focused their initial efforts on involving and engaging the diverse many in sales in helping with integration initiatives alongside a deliberate focus on culture. That started almost immediately after the deal was finalized and passed government review.

In this case, both firms had done many acquisitions over the years, and there was considerable groaning about what people anticipated was forthcoming. But the CEO, COO, and new head of sales chose an approach that was different than that used many times before, an approach consistent with the principles, processes, playbooks, and emerging science of change described in this book.

The new head of the combined salesforce believed that she needed this merger to be led by her people, not managed and controlled by others above them. And she needed her people to act in new one-team ways which produced better than expected results, and quickly.

She had senior leaders come together to articulate a vision of the future, emphasizing realistic and emotionally compelling opportunities available to them as the undeniable industry leader. This opportunity, paired with clarity of what success would look like (i.e. ability to sell both legacy companies' products, taking the best of each company's sales processes, increased market share, and increased sales of their most profitable products) served as a guide for the entire effort.

Diverse teams were created with membership from both legacy organizations. Each team had a specific focus. One built a broad sense of urgency around the opportunity by creating a mechanism for two-way dialogue between employees and leadership; focusing on removing distracting (Survive-inducing) barriers to success (such as the lack of a collated email distribution list to enable communication between the newly merged sales teams); and providing opportunities for live and virtual touchpoints to build a sense of community and awareness between two legacy teams.

Other groups channeled building urgency into meaningful action that demonstrated the new one-team way of working was both possible (cynics did not believe this at all) and much more effective. One team was specifically focused on innovation (a critical element of Thrive that is often ignored during M&A integration). This blue-sky team found ways to leverage their professional and social networks to drive sales for their most profitable products in ways they had never attempted before. Throughout the process, they were given permission and support from leadership to test and iterate, creating a microcosm of a culture of innovation and collaboration that later became central to the combined entity. Another team focused more on the nitty-gritty, such as training on new systems and combined products. The training was done in a way that limited the common slowdown and loss of productivity associated with M&A (which helped mitigate overheated Survive).

These strategic initiatives—led by employees at all levels, not senior management—drove new action, better results, communication, and celebration. Within months, it was clear this merger was going to be different from their other M&A experiences. New mindsets emerged, then habits, then the beginning of a new single sales culture—all done faster, with less pain, and more short-term successes.

As the actual success within sales was communicated by individuals throughout the new firm, cooperation, new action, teamwork, wins, celebration, and so on grew elsewhere in the enterprise. And while some industry analysts predicted that a disruptive year or two would inevitably cost them short-term market share, on some key measures, during the first two years market share actually went up (as it did, for example, on the list of best selling items in their industry). Innovation actually went up. Survive-driven disruption was not zero—it probably never is in the best of these cases—but it was much below expectations. Said one early skeptic, "If I had not seen this with my own eyes, if I had just read propaganda pieces from corporate communications, I would never have believed what happened. Never."

Given all the M&A activity we might reasonably expect over the coming decade, the stakes again stand out starkly. We can continue to do this work as we have been. More likely, we can continue to learn a bit and improve the deal and integration process somewhat. Or we can much more relentlessly and aggressively use what we have learned through change research.

Unlocking Value: The Demerger Issue

The logic of M&A rests on the belief that the value of merged organizations will be greater than the sum of the parts. There is a corollary to this logic, which states that in some cases the value of parts will be greater than the whole.

Sometime in the 1970s, a group of people, many from academia, developed the idea that large enterprises often contained trapped economic value because of the way that they were put together through internal expansion of products and services, growth into new geographies, acquisitions, and mergers. Further, they argued that unlocking that wasted value was relatively simple. It just required the willpower to sell off parts of the business, perhaps including recent acquisitions, to shut parts down, or to demerge. Done correctly, the market value of the parts would exceed the value of the original firm, sometimes by a considerable amount. Considering the results of so many M&A deals, it is not difficult to imagine why this might be true.

Our reading of history does not show where this concept was first tested. But clearly in the 1980s and 1990s, a number of efforts—usually to unlock economic value by breaking up conglomerates built in the 1960s and 1970s—were successful financially. Today, we occasionally see raiders or big institutional investors pushing management to sell/shut/split and the theory of the case is borne out again. We also increasingly see technology (and non-tech) companies splitting to create more nimble, flexible entities. Done sensibly, the parts are immediately worth more in the stock market than the old whole.

In a world demanding more agility, innovation, and speed, having value capabilities locked into a firm, where they are not being capitalized upon, is increasingly a risky proposition. Certainly, there will continue to be cases where the best answer is a divestiture. That will be the sensible way to change and be more competitive, more valuable, more able to produce great products and services, or more able to grow revenues and jobs. But there is another way to think about locked-in value, and a whole different approach to releasing innovation and creativity.

We are talking about cases where competitively useful ideas and the power to execute those ideas successfully and swiftly is locked in.

In such cases, what is trapped is human energy, human intellect, and the human capacity to take advantage of those big opportunities. Here the lock is not the result of legal glue that holds a group of businesses together. It is misshapen bureaucracy, out-of-date policies, historical culture, top-down-only approaches to change issues, and certain mindsets of people, all of which easily develops as firms grow and mature. But one consequence of this development is under-activated Thrive. So good ideas, and peoples' capacity to execute those ideas quickly, are not available to help organizations flourish. Activate and guide the right process, and the creative, energized, rapid execution potential can be unlocked, with especially powerful benefits today and even more so in the foreseeable future.

To be clear, we are not talking about well-known human relations or human resource or employee engagement strategies, the oldest of which date back to the 1950s and the newest to the last decade or two. The key here is not just creating a more pleasant working environment with architecture and free lunches, or starting to treat people as if they really were intelligent and motivated creatures, or removing layers of stifling management (or bosses altogether), or a few interdepartmental task forces and innovation committees. It is not what is often called a "skunk works" or the offering of economic incentives for innovative ideas or their execution. Elements from many or all of these approaches might be relevant and helpful in specific situations. But none of these approaches is the key to effectively releasing untapped potential.

The key of which we speak is a different approach to changing organizations than is the norm today. It is the approach described in this book. It includes a "dual system" of sorts that focuses on management processes to achieve reliable, consistent performance and on the leadership behaviors and participation from many that is required to unleash innovation and effective change generally. It is an approach that acts with a realistic understanding of some core components of human nature, which sees most modern organizations for what they are (early Industrial Age creatures that struggle with rapid change), and which appreciates the logic of the research-found pattern of mobilizing large and diverse groups of people to want to change because their hearts are in it, and who do successfully change their enterprises by providing proactive aligned leadership. (We will have more to say on "dual systems" in Chapter 8 on Agile methodologies.)

It is hard to measure meaningfully how much value, which could benefit many, is locked into organizations today. But any informed guess produces massive numbers.

The point here is that to deal well with a rapidly changing context, filled with more uncertainties, we not only need to pass on some deals because cultural integration under the best of circumstances will take too much time—time you simply do not have. We also need to start passing on the selling side of M&A activity because there is a better way to unlock value.

To be clear, we are not suggesting that divestitures or spin-offs are never the right answer, rather that there is an alternative to unlocking value. We are talking about a methodology that does take some time to complete, but that has the potential to produce much better results. Over the longer term, this approach can create organizations that are able to compete and win in a 100-mph world—a world where all companies—not just the smaller, fast-growing ones—need to be agile in the face of change.

Chapter 8

Agile Methodologies That Build Sustained and Scalable Agility

"**A**gile" methodologies for helping enterprises adapt to a faster-moving and more demanding world came from software development in the late 1990s and early 2000s, although their roots probably go back as far as the 1950s. As we write this, Agile is still most often leveraged for software development, although it is "scaling"—that is, moving beyond software to other parts of enterprises. This evolution to broader applications looks somewhat the same as when "quality circles," "continuous improvement," and "Six Sigma" started in manufacturing/factories and then migrated elsewhere, or as "design thinking" started in product design and has now been tried across functions and industries.

It is easy to see why Agile has become fashionable. In a more unpredictable and rapidly changing world, it logically follows that you need more agility. And it is easy to posit a logic for why it started in software development.

By the 1990s, all medium and large firms had serious, expensive IT functions that had experience in going from one generation to the next of hardware or software. More often than not, those experiences were painful. Transitions took too long. Projects exceeded already sizable budgets. Sometimes enterprises simply failed and had to start over.

Back then, IT sometimes seemed like a budgetary black hole. Work often appeared to move at 15 miles an hour, which created pain both inside and outside IT. And that pain created a demand that led to a 4-point manifesto and 12 principles that defined a different way to develop software, with a greater emphasis on responsiveness to customer needs, and less focus on rigid, process-driven plans.

The Agile Manifesto and principles have a lot of validity. For example, if marketing asks for a different sort of customer management system software, you don't assign an IT team to work in a conference room for months and months and only have them show it to marketing after the system is up and running. Experience shows that marketing will be upset not only about how long it took but also how much it cost. Even more so, they will have needs and suggestions, uncommunicated or unrecognized at the beginning of the project, which will require more than a small amount of rework. Solution: Agile Principle #4, "close daily cooperation between business people and developers." In this case, have some marketing people on the team from the beginning, which will enable them to spot problems and opportunities earlier, and thus correction or capitalization will occur when it is still easy and fast to do. Buy-in and adoption also tends to increase—often dramatically—when end-user input is taken into account from the outset.

Because of a fair degree of face validity, and because of the sheer pressure from the business environment to develop software today faster, better, and cheaper, some Agile ideas have made their way into virtually all large companies and many medium-sized firms. In big companies in particular, you can usually find a software initiative or two (or even more) that has come close to really embracing Agile and achieved impressive results. But even in those cases, the success formula has rarely spread to become the software development norm in the firms involved, much less sustainable organization-wide norms beyond software that fosters agility.

Indeed, if you look at the initial press Agile received at the turn of the twenty-first century, the gap between prediction and promise, versus today's reality, is a large one—despite the pressures to move faster to cope with a more complicated world. In light of the emerging science of change, this outcome is not surprising.

Why Agile Does Not Create Sustained or Scaled Agility

Implementing Agile methodology, as it is too often done today, is not the same as becoming agile. The fundamental problem is that Agile Principles are not consistent with the basic design of modern organizations. So it is easy for Agile Principles to be overtaken by rigid and detailed managerial processes—losing the intent and results those principles were meant to produce.

Remember, the large enterprises that began to emerge in significant numbers a century and a half ago were created to produce and distribute products at unprecedented scale without the enterprise falling into confusion, chaos, intolerable inefficiencies, and the like. The whole design leans toward methods that foster predictability, stability, and order to create reliable product quality and healthy financial results.

So, for example, Agile Principle #2 is "Welcome changing requirements, even in late development." But planning discipline is central to the modern organizational form. Good planning is done thoroughly at the outset, and then executed. It is not done, then redone when new requirements emerge, then redone again when more new requirements come along. The latter is disruptive, inefficient, confusing, and thus unacceptable. Even in organizations that claim to embrace Agile's "fail-fast," "minimum viable product" (MVP) essence, one rarely sees leaders providing air cover to teams trying to implement this way of working despite the barriers. Human nature and the modern organizational form are more powerful forces on senior management than the logic and usefulness of Agile.

Of course, a strong leader, some enthusiastic people, or even some desperation can overcome natural, built-in organizational barriers and *force* an Agile approach. But as soon as the leader, high enthusiasm, or desperation goes away, the organization tends to reassert its natural form and the Agile methodology starts to wane. Questions arise about the details of an initial plan, sometimes demanding answers to every possible contingency. Instead of being praised for getting an MVP out the door, teams are penalized for imperfections in initial output. All this starts to raise alarm bells, and shuts down the Thrive-activated speed and innovation that Agile is intended to foster. The same sort of phenomena occurred with many efforts at installing Six Sigma, Design Thinking, or other potentially powerful approaches that came on strong, were "adopted" by large numbers of organizations, peaked, then began to lose momentum, and struggled with sustainability.

So, is sustainable and scaled Agile impossible? It is impossible with the primary organizational form found in the world today. But that is not the only way one can set up and run a significant modern enterprise.

A Dual Systems Approach

Somewhere around 2012, we discovered in our research and practice that organizations tend to go through a metamorphosis as they age that is similar to, but still different from, conventional notions about enterprise life cycles.

Specifically, enterprises tend to be born looking not at all like a modern organization. Formal planning systems, budgets, carefully drawn organization charts, metrics, and control systems, as well as formal policies and the like are all essentially missing. For the bank, if a loan is needed, or for the angel investor, if money is to be raised that way, entrepreneurs will put on paper something that reads like a conventional modern organization. But in reality, it is mostly fantasy.

Young firms do not operate with rigid formal hierarchies. They operate more like loosely knit networks, without a great deal of management. But successful cases demonstrate aligned leadership, usually coming strongly from one or two people with a little more of the same from many around them. Formal policies and systems and reports are rare.

To a large degree, young successful enterprises, especially in the tech world, operate by Agile Principles. And these firms behave with agility, with initiatives coming and going, and the shape of the network and peoples' place in it shifting regularly. Nearly everyone is engaged. The strength of the system is its capacity to adapt, move quickly, innovate, and in general change with evolving knowledge and requirements.

But with success and growth and scale comes the need to manage and control. Early on, a node somewhere on the network starts to develop a different structure and process. Within this node, or sometimes more than one node, the structure is hierarchical. The process is more managerial. Systems and policies slowly start to emerge. And with growth, this new aspect of the organization starts taking on a larger and larger role.

In all successful organizations, there is a period of time when both systems are operating together—a dual system—each focused on different goals. The original entrepreneurial/leadership network tends to activate Thrive and to drive innovation, speed, adaptability, and change. The new hierarchy connects more with our Survive side and drives efficiency, problem-solving, reliability, and stability. This dual arrangement is often not visible because one part is formal and explicit and the other more informal and implicit. And these are not two separate departments, staffed by different people. Most of the same managers and employees work both sides, often one as a "day job" (usually the hierarchy) and one as a "side gig" (usually the network).

Because the two systems are so different, the potential for conflict is inherent.

A DUAL OPERATING SYSTEM THAT ENABLES AGILE PRINCIPLES

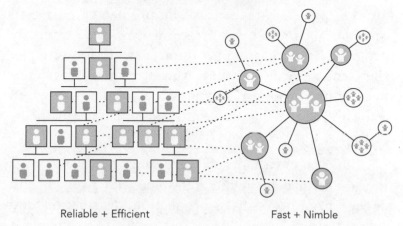

Reliable + Efficient   Fast + Nimble

In some cases, the original entrepreneurial network limits the natural and needed growth of the management hierarchy and systems. People in the former see the latter as a threat to their freedom, as undermining their ability to innovate, and decry the horrors of bureaucracy. This sort of fight can continue for some time, with the original system dominating until the negative consequences caused by inefficiencies and chaos overwhelm.

In other cases, the management hierarchy takes over prematurely. Those in charge talk of the need for growing up. "We are no longer five people operating out of a garage and we have to stop acting as if we are." But with the agile network arrangement beaten down, more often than not, innovation and growth slow.

In the most successful enterprises we have studied, the two systems work for a while in tandem with a variety of mechanisms mediating natural conflict. It helps that the same people play a role both in what becomes an informal network and in the management hierarchy. You don't find the "us-versus-them" and silo problems we have all experienced. It also helps greatly when people explicitly recognize how they are operating. It helps, for example, when senior executives have learned that their job is sometimes to be a "sponsor" for network-based initiatives, to deal with barriers that the teams cannot handle by themselves, and then to get out of the way.

But even in virtually all "successful" businesses, over time the management hierarchy becomes stronger and bigger, out of necessity, as production, distribution, and administration demands grow and grow. At some point, it is not unusual for the management processes to crush the entrepreneurial network. The firm emerges as a mature, more slowly growing, not at all agile enterprise.

In the past, in a slower world, even "overmanaged and under-led" organizations could perform adequately by the standards of the day if they had some source of strength: strong brand recognition, high market share and economies of scale, key patents, or a unique global presence. With some modification, where network-like task forces are added to drive initiatives, survival was secure. But today, increasingly small tweaks to the single system that runs mature modern organizations is not enough to create the agility, adaptability, and speed needed to compete and win. What is needed is that dual system that all big organizations once had, if only briefly, early in their histories.

When the dual system becomes just a part of "how we do things here"—that is, as it sinks into the culture—you get sustainable agility. You create an environment where it is actually possible to implement Agile Principles the way they were intended—leading to a more adaptable organization that gets things done faster. You end up with a situation that is not dependent on one unusually capable boss to push through new and better ways to handle strategy, digital transformation, restructuring, culture, or M&A. You have new and better methods for dealing with change that do not fade away when a great boss moves on. We mean, of course, methods such as a bias toward a select few *and* diverse many, toward using have to *and* want to, engaging head *and* heart, demonstrating vigilance about threats *and* opportunities, and the like. You also have an operating model that is more consistent with, and supportive of, Agile Principles. A network, with its good working relationships across departmental silos, for example, is the perfect mechanism to consistently apply Agile Principle #4: "Close daily cooperation between business people and developers."

A dual system in the culture yields an organization that allows both Survive and Thrive to do what they were designed to do without overheating or going to sleep—all of which helps create an enterprise that is *sustainably* reliable, efficient, fast, and agile.

It Is Not Just about Software Development

This dual system applies in general today. It goes way beyond just software development. Scaled and

Sustainable Agile requires an agile network structure built into the entire organization, and with it more leadership built in everywhere, yet without abandoning management and hierarchy.

We have seen dual systems provide agility not only in IT but in sales organizations, not only in high tech, but low tech too, not only in the U.S., but worldwide. Dual systems can help support new and better ways to form and execute strategy in a rapidly changing world. They can help with restructuring, cultural renewal, M&A, and digital transformation.

To some degree, dual systems better mirror the dual design of human nature than the modern conventional organizational form. With hierarchy more adept at dealing with immediate threats and networks more capable of capitalizing on novel opportunities, dual systems make it easier to mobilize masses and provide a platform for more leadership than the conventional form.

And—this is the big point—once locked into place because it's just seen as "the way we do things here" (that is, it's in the culture), a dual system makes short-term efficiency and reliability as well as longer-term agility and innovation sustainable.

Building a Dual System: An Example

"It has sustained itself for seven years now," he tells us, "which is remarkable since most of the people here thought it would last one year at most. We had a history of 'flavors of the month' activities where we launched projects, task forces, and programs, perhaps had some initial success, yet failed to sustain. But not in this case."

He works in an 80-year-old business that was started in wholesaling for some big-ticket consumer items. After initially establishing itself as a successful, growing enterprise, the firm expanded by aggressively buying small, local mom-and-pop wholesalers in their industry and then letting them operate with some autonomy. The organization evolved over its first 65 years, but slowly and very incrementally. No one would have dreamed of calling it a tech business.

Change has sped up in the last decade due to a variety of new forces, including digital disruption, the need to better integrate all the acquisitions, and the opportunity to merge with newer online retailers. During this time, the company has prospered by adopting a dual system, changing more, moving faster, and in general becoming more agile.

The nerve center of the dual system is a "guiding coalition," a core team that coordinates the activities of the network and ensures integration with the hierarchy. In this case, the 2019 guiding coalition (GC) comprised 60 people who were selected from 189 applicants. This group of volunteers represented each department and geographic area and consisted of individuals with great diversity, passion, connections within the business, and initiative.

The GCs had a tenure of one year and each year's group incorporated the learnings from previous years. The senior leaders demonstrated their commitment and willingness to invest in the teams by supporting a "kick-off" event over multiple days at corporate headquarters. Top executives participated in the event, providing their perspective about the state of the business and even pitching ideas (which the GCs would be free to choose or not) about what they felt could be powerful strategic initiatives for moving the business forward.

Through an open and transparent brainstorming session, in 2019 the team identified nearly forty potential initiatives. Some were about sales and growth, others about operational efficiency, others about digital or technical issues, and some about culture and employee relations.

They had learned that the network functions best when a diverse group of individuals work on projects that they feel passionate about. Therefore, a critical role of their GCs was to match people with projects. That same year the team narrowed down the initial project list to the 14 with the most energy behind them (i.e. individuals with activated Thrive willing to lead the project) and which most strongly connected to the overall business opportunities. The end result was seven action teams, each comprising approximately seven members and focused on two initiatives per team.

A key principle behind the activities of their network is that the teams make their own decisions on how to realize the opportunity in each initiative. Each team devised their own metrics and their own action plans. To keep activities coordinated and to help remove barriers, the teams reported monthly to key executives. Once a quarter, they met face to face. Recognizing the need to celebrate and generate excitement around participating in this work, a big face-to-face report out was scheduled at the end of the year—a celebration and, in essence, a "graduation."

Interdepartmental or business unit politics was not totally absent in the networked activities, but it was low. People acted as unified teams with an openness and candor that was not typical in the organization (or in virtually any large modern organization). Busy people rarely dropped the ball in their initiatives or on their "regular" jobs. The diversity within teams more often led to creativity, not unproductive conflict. Bosses rarely shut down activity with smothering controls or demands, and some stepped up to aggressively remove barriers that the networked teams could not figure out how to remove by themselves. As a result, useful initiatives were identified, pursued, and executed both in a volume and at a speed that is simply not "natural" in modern hierarchical, management-focused organizations.

While the network did its work, the regular hierarchy continued to focus on buying, selling, warehousing, collections, and all the many tasks needed to run the business each day, week, quarter. The network, including the core group of 60 and hundreds of others who were mobilized to work on specific tasks or projects, helped the firm change, improve, and move ahead, with agility, into an always shifting future.

"We are not perfect, let me be clear," one of those intimately involved in their dual system told us recently. "But I am often asked by people I know who don't work here how we have managed to do this. I think typically it sounds too good to be really true. So, anyway, I have thought about that question and I think there are two reasons that are particularly important.

"First, we sought out good expertise in helping us set this system up and, as a result, we started actually getting things done, that were important to the business, faster and better than people expected. The GC that first year was maybe 30 people (we were a smaller organization). Nevertheless, the very first year we successfully addressed a chronic business issue that had been slowing growth for years and years. That was crucial because it began quickly to win over a lot of skeptics and caught the attention of the executive committee, especially the new COO.

"Second, and related to the first reason this has worked so well, a few key executives, including the COO, once they saw the logic and power of what was happening became real champions, so when we hit natural bumps—political, bureaucratic, interpersonal—they did not hesitate to take action that would smooth the way.

"And the overall business results speak for themselves. We have added additional wholesale brands. We have better integrated acquisitions. Our foray into digital retail is working. We have maintained or added to our strong competitive position. And we have grown a lot.

"On the more personal side, there are some people who have worked on the GCs along the way who will tell you that it was the best work, or the best developmental experience, they have been involved in within their entire careers."

Here, and in similar cases in which we have been involved or researched, human nature and modern organizational tendencies pushed heavily against the formation of a functioning sustained scaled agile system. Formal hierarchies and management systems tend to naturally throw up barriers of all sorts. Modern organizations are inclined to turn leadership networks into check-the-box, highly standardized activities that do not activate Thrive, unleash innovative energy, mobilize people, and thus accomplish much—which makes it easier to kill them off.

But, bottom line, there is no question that attention to those forces, keeping Survive from overactivating, and revving up Thrive, with the lessons learned from leading change and brain research, can create twenty first century dual-systems organizations, where sustainable agility across the enterprise continues to achieve hard-to-imagine results at hard-to-believe speeds.

Chapter 9

Broad Social Initiatives That Can Help Billions

There is another, even broader, consequence to more rapid and complex change. In addition to the need for almost all organizations to adapt, adjust, accelerate, and get ahead of the curve, we collectively face perils and have wonderful possibilities that transcend what any single enterprise can handle. The perils include climate disasters, unexpected pandemics, man made chemical/biological/nuclear vehicles of mass destruction, and systemic racism. The possibilities include all sorts of improvements in public health, from the elimination of deadly diseases to the easing of suffering at a massive level.

Avoiding the perils and taking advantage of the opportunities requires action from many individuals who are not necessarily part of any unified organization. Fighting diseases, eliminating poverty, addressing political movements—these all require challenging the status quo and mobilizing significant support from a diverse groundswell of individuals and organizations.

We tend to think of all these efforts as social causes that have little in common with corporate strategy exercises, restructurings, mergers and acquisitions, and the other topics discussed in this book. *But while there are some differences in the details, these causes face many of the same potential pitfalls as corporate change and can benefit from many of the same solutions.*

Ultimately, it is all about our ability to lead change in a complex and increasingly changing world, to survive and thrive despite the multitude of barriers. The complexities certainly can vary greatly depending on the threat or opportunity, and on the number of people and organizations involved. But at some level, the dynamics of producing meaningful change—the problems and solutions—are always the same because human nature is human nature, modern organizations are modern organizations, and the world really is becoming more and more interconnected with a rate of change and level of uncertainty that is unprecedented.

So what does the research on change inside organizations tell us about social change involving large systems of enterprises, groups, individuals, governments, and more?

Quite a bit, actually.

Lessons from Organizational Research

To review briefly, the three most important lessons we have learned about prospering in a more rapidly changing world are these.

First, unlike even a century ago, life is now driven in so many ways by large formal modern organizations—and they have been designed primarily for efficiency and reliability, not for innovation and speedy change.

These enterprises are a very new phenomenon, unknown for 99.99% of the time that *Homo sapiens* have roamed the earth. No longer does a small family or tribe provide housing, food, healthcare, safety, and all sorts of other products and services to its own members. These needs are now served by a multitude of formal organizations that evolved after the industrial revolution and are designed around a hierarchy of jobs and managerial processes. This organizational form was invented of necessity to take advantage of the industrial revolution and the possibilities of much larger-scale production and distribution of better goods at lower prices. In this design, efficiency, reliability, and stability were key goals, while constant innovation, change, and agility were not.

Because of ever-growing interconnectedness among enterprises and nations, social change is impossible without the help of lots of these organizations—not just businesses, but governments, NGOs, foundations, and more. Though in some ways there is much diversity here, all these entities are based on the modern, century-old form, which, with its emphasis on standardization and stability, easily serves up a great many barriers to change of significance. Any single enterprise can throw up dozens of difficult barriers.

But with social change, we are not talking about single organizations. We are literally speaking of tens, hundreds, or thousands of government units, businesses, and foundations, and hundreds of thousands or millions of people who need to collaborate or act in some new ways. This scale of cooperation is not intuitive to human nature.

Thus, it is not total hyperbole to say that the challenge facing big social change efforts can be like trying to move most of the Rocky Mountains to Tennessee. And in many cases, the biggest obstacle to making more progress on these wildly difficult goals is the fact that those involved often greatly underestimate this reality about the sheer magnitude of the task.

A second (more encouraging) lesson from change research is that truly remarkable results are possible.

Even inherently optimistic people can completely surprise themselves in terms of what they and their organizations can accomplish with the right understanding of how to go about complex change in a rapidly moving world. That understanding starts with an appreciation of the necessity for and power of diverse masses, who want something to happen because their hearts are in it, and who make a difference by helping to lead change.

These are people whose Thrive Channel is activated and many of whom help activate Thrive in others. These are people who take new action, and encourage others to take it, which achieves better results—results that are recognized and communicated and celebrated. That, in turn, helps foster more action, more results, and growing momentum until changed mindsets start to emerge. Then eventually come changed habits, then new norms, values, and hence culture, which helps make change truly sustainable.

Focusing on building momentum in this way is as relevant, if not more so, in social versus organizational change. When the focus instead slides to an all-or-nothing approach, and does not create or celebrate successes along the way, large-scale social initiatives can struggle to make headway beyond endless talk.

A third major lesson from our organizational work is that people totally underestimate the power of the Survive system that is hardwired into all of us.

Leaders, managers, and employees miss how often they try to make change happen, yet fail to do so because they inadvertently overactivate Survive, create anxiety and anger, and stress out others and sometimes themselves. Overheated Survive then swamps the Thrive impulse needed to bring about agility, innovation, adaptation, and change.

This problem is even more acute within the context of social change where the threats faced often permeate all aspects of life, both personal and professional. Furthermore, in some cases the threats can be very much directed at physical safety, which triggers an immediate and strong Survive response, easily overwhelming Thrive.

The solution here is not to turn overactivated Survive into underactivated Survive, to go "from Survive to Thrive." Even very sophisticated people fall into this trap both while trying to make their enterprises prosper and while attempting to drive broad-scale social change. What's needed is a healthy and appropriate activation of both Survive and Thrive.

Broad-Scale Social Change: Wonderful—and Disappointing

We have not done sufficient research to say with confidence what the norms are today for big social change initiatives. But from what we have seen, even "success" cases too often leave people disappointed.

And there are many successes. One can find a remarkable track record over the last few centuries in driving down infant and maternal deaths, in reducing unbearable poverty, in greatly increasing literacy, in improving the quality of life, and in curtailing violence and warfare. Yet despite this reality, it is easy to find stories from the recent past that are discouraging in their outcomes and, even more so, in the missed opportunity to make faster and better progress.

Here's a typical example. A consortium consisting of a UN agency, a major foundation, a few NGOs, and a couple of businesses makes a joint commitment to wipe out worldwide new cases of a certain disease. This is a terrible malady for which there is no cure but there is a vaccine, and it is not very expensive.

A committee puts together a plan with clear timelines, responsibilities, budgets, and policies for how the work will be done. The effort is launched with press fanfare.

Bureaucracy and politics both among and within the participating organizations creep into the process from the start. Nevertheless, some dedicated people and generous funding drive results that are carefully measured on a country-by-country basis. Within 5 years, progress is clearly being made. Within 10 years they are in sight of their goal of no new cases. And then, mostly because of epidemics in only a few countries, the numbers stop going down and actually start going up. Sadly, it becomes clear that they will miss their target completion date.

So the committee develops a new plan and creates a new budget. Money is taken away from some players and reallocated to existing organizations and a few new ones. The donor agency that is providing the most funding tries to convince the group that a better governance structure is needed to hold people accountable. The structure they have in mind gives less power to the U.N. agency. The agency resists and wins that battle.

Implementation begins again with a goal of eliminating new cases of the disease in five years. Progress is made in year one, less in year two. Explanations of why this is happening vary depending upon whom one asks. Some say the people in charge have been naive from day one regarding the difficulty of making anything happen in a few poor and war-wrecked countries. Some say the task is doable but the need to keep the money coming is a significant, perverse incentive that is slowing victory (which would end the distribution of funds). Some say that it is all about governance and accountability. And still others point fingers at certain key players whom they believe are simply not equipped for the work.

At the end of year five, they miss their target a second time.

Incredibly, in a world where money can dry up very quickly if targets are missed, the funding agency does not quit. But it does hire a well-known consulting firm to look into the situation and offer analysis and advice. The consultants conduct interviews and collect a lot of data. People maneuver to avoid blame and to position themselves for continued involvement. The consultants write a long report recommending a new governance structure—which, yes, does align closely with the beliefs of the funding agency.

Plan three is launched with a new governance structure and a more explicit hierarchy of authority and responsibilities. The new timetable says victory comes in three years.

It does not.

Why? Some very smart people were involved. There was generous funding. A known medical solution was available.

Supporters would say that what they did accomplish was extraordinary and it certainly had an impact on many millions of lives. Is this not victory? Critics retort that the opportunity cost in time (many years) and money (billions of dollars) dedicated to this one initiative was too high in a world with so many other needs. Critics also say a sustainable solution is essential. That begins by stopping all new cases, because the world is so interdependent that failure in even a single country threatens everyone. Also needed is a well-designed contingency plan to spot any subsequent flare-up immediately so as to deal with it when it is small and relatively easy to contain.

These points are well taken. What is indisputable is that achieving the results quicker and with fewer resources employed is dearly needed—not only in this one case, but many like it, where the focus is narrow, the time and resources employed are very big, and the opportunities ignored in the process are large.

What is striking to us is how much the basic approach used in this case to a very large-scale change is similar to the norm in single enterprises today, and how much it produces most of the same unwanted effects.

This global health initiative utilized data-driven managerial processes, without the early engagement of large numbers who wanted to make this happen because their hearts were in it, without sufficient Thrive-activation, and without remotely enough people taking the lead in making things happen in thousands and thousands of locations around the world.

Perhaps even more so than in organizational change, social change is ripe for engaging the many, tapping into their emotional connection to a cause, and galvanizing want-to-based action. But that did not happen here. As a result, the elites on top did not have sufficient and timely information on what was occurring in nearly 200 countries. Even if they had, how could they have processed that information, made centralized decisions, and successfully directed enough others to act?

A relatively small number of select people had to deal with thousands of governmental units from across the globe, yet their understanding of the culture and politics and history and quirks in all those organizations and communities was very limited. Consequently, they were making decisions all the time that inevitably were going to run into barriers. They were taking actions that seemed rational but that were triggering parochial politics, rumors, fear of the unknown, and then overheated Survive responses, especially in some of the most challenging countries.

The centralized decision-making also made it impossible to react quickly to new information about what was changing, evolving, working, or not working—when, for example, a communication campaign was not being received well or when a procurement and supply chain needed to respond to some new political reality.

True, it is amazing they achieved what they did. But much can be accomplished with a sort of brute force if you have smart people, proven technology, and many resources. However, given the scale of the challenges facing humanity, this brute-force approach is not sufficient. We need smarter, faster, more resource-effective, and more sustainable solutions.

Was there really an alternative? Success stories, when you can find them, suggest there is. And it will sound familiar to readers of this book.

#1. Diverse masses of people are inspired to take opportunity-based action, with a real sense of urgency, because they want to make something happen. Their hearts are deeply in it. The Thrive side of their human nature is well activated.

Probably the best examples of inspiring diverse masses are the various successful political movements that even in the face of highly stacked odds, came out on top. What all of these movements have in common is that they find ways to activate Thrive even in the midst of immense challenge or crisis. They may employ humor and pranks, as in the Otpor movement to overthrow Slobodan Milošević in Serbia. Or political movements may engage the compelling visions of a better future, as in post-apartheid South Africa, triggering positive emotions of joy, belonging, and enthusiasm, which are critical to activating and sustaining action.

#2. To a degree, management and controls and small elite groups and funding are relevant, not least as a force both to support action and to keep it from swinging into chaos. In fact, the lack of an ability to establish functioning processes, essentially management and control, is a key factor in the less-than-ideal outcomes of many political movements. One example is the Arab Spring, where in many cases the vacuum created from the changes instigated by the movement was filled with something other than what the founding members of the movement would have wanted. Nevertheless, centering the whole organizing force around management and controls, as a frustrated group increasingly did in the case of the vaccine, is not the solution.

#3. Pushing for change from a small controlling group will never work as well as a pull from a broad group that is inspired to want to see change happen. Hierarchy and analytics are neither the spark that catalyzes change nor the key energy source that can create seeming miracles that benefit humanity.

An example that provides real optimism for what is possible, even when navigating global complexity, is the effort to reverse the depletion of the ozone layer that started in the late 1980s.

The ozone "shield," discovered by two French physicists in 1913, was subsequently found to filter out 97 to 99% of the Sun's medium-frequency ultraviolet light, which, if it reached the surface of earth, could do irreparable harm to human life. In 1976, it was found that this protective shield was being depleted.

A compelling visual (although scientifically inaccurate) of an ozone hole, combined with an easy-to-understand benefit, helped inspire voluntary action from citizens. This action created urgency that led to a global treaty—the Montreal Protocol—calling for a ban on chlorofluorocarbons even before there was complete scientific consensus about the scale of the problem and its cause.

As of this writing, the ozone hole is the smallest it has been since its discovery. The world is on track to meet the target of returning the ozone layer to its 1980 levels, which will be a monumental accomplishment.

Due to its widespread adoption and implementation, the Montreal Protocol has been hailed as "perhaps the single most successful international agreement to date."

The success of the Montreal treaty has been at least partially attributed to the involvement of stakeholders early in the negotiations. Scientists, the chemical industry, and governments were part of the discussions that led to the treaty. Additionally, by starting with modest goals and demonstrating early success, momentum kept building and the initial targets were revised upward multiple times, eventually resulting in a call for near 100% reduction in the damaging chemicals.

These examples illustrate that the same basic dynamic that creates accelerated, adaptive, successful strategic change inside organizations can also create it across organizations. Some differences in language help hide the similarities, since with large-scale social initiatives one rarely if ever speaks of "M&A" or "sustainable scaled agile." Even "cultural renewal," "restructuring," and "strategy" are not central ideas in this arena. Terms like "policy development," "partnership management," or "governance structure," all of which can sound non-corporate, in fact hide the fact that the challenges and solutions are similar in both the single organization and social initiative arenas because, at heart, it is all about large-scale, complex change in human systems.

A "Social Movement"

Large-scale social change is sometimes talked about in terms of inspiring a social movement. Many of the examples mentioned above fall into this category.

On the surface, social movements seem to be completely different from corporate efforts to strategize, transform digitally, restructure, and so on. Yet some of the most remarkable change efforts we have witnessed inside single organizations were very much centered around the creation of a well-led social movement.

When enough people from enough places start providing some leadership around a shared sense of an opportunity to make their world better, and do so with a positive emotional set, you have the beginnings of a social movement. If they concentrate on visible results, seen and communicated and celebrated, momentum will build. The same is true whether the topic is overthrowing a despotic regime, reducing poverty across a country, or digital transformation at one city's newspaper.

Of course, there are significant differences between, for example, a big restructuring initiative at an automotive manufacturer and a social movement to bring about change in the rights available to a marginalized population. What we are saying is that basic mistakes that undermine success are nevertheless often the same in all these settings, as are some of the basic forces for success.

Social movements and development projects could learn important lessons by studying corporate change efforts. Likewise, companies could learn something useful by studying development projects and social movements. It goes both ways.

For example, social movements initially struggle with the challenge of building sufficient urgency among a broad enough group of people to gain momentum. The findings from corporate change efforts emphasize the importance of articulating an opportunity statement that is forward looking and positively focused. For corporations this means more focus, for example, on what a restructuring effort will enable them to achieve and less about the problems in the current situation. The same principles apply for social movements; acknowledge the current reality, then focus on the dream of a better future.

Corporations have figured out how to "manage" change, at least to some extent. This includes ensuring there are adequate systems, processes, and metrics to coordinate work, keep initiatives from flying destructively out of control, and to honestly evaluate success or the lack thereof. Social movements, except those that are very narrowly focused on a singular easy-to-measure goal, can benefit from more of these systems and metrics.

In the case of development projects, in many ways these are very similar to corporate change efforts. The tactics we have been discussing in this book are equally applicable, just with more stakeholders to engage and a correspondingly greater need for coordination.

Corporate change efforts, on the other hand, can also benefit from studying the tactics used by successful social movements to create engagement and participation. For example, many movements have succeeded through a model of escalating commitment. This is why you receive all those political emails asking you to show support by signing a petition. The small commitment of signing a petition will often lead to larger ones, like making a donation or volunteering your time.

Social movements are also adept at emotional messaging that speaks to the heart. Business leaders would benefit from speaking more to the heart, in addition to the head.

A Social Movement Around Leadership

One could argue that of all the social movements needed in the world today, none might be more important in the long run than one that teaches humanity how to better deal with a more swiftly moving, more uncertain, and increasingly complex world. If we can do that, we put ourselves in a much better position to successfully address all of the other challenges we face across the globe, from ensuring access to healthcare, food, and housing, to addressing climate change and creating a more inclusive and equitable world. That approach would require a lot of change, starting with very basic notions about what leadership is and whose job it is to help provide that leadership. Is it even possible to imagine a rallying cry of "millions leading, billions benefiting?"

Given the way that almost everyone has been taught to think about leadership, the honest answer to our question from many quarters is probably "no". *Nevertheless, best evidence suggests that when it comes to change, it really is all about leadership.*

Part III

IN THE END, IT IS MOSTLY ABOUT THIS

Chapter 10

More Leadership from More People

Reflecting on the disappointments and occasional grand successes that organizations are having in accelerating needed change using various methodologies, including the most common ones described in this book, no single lesson comes across as clearly as one related to leadership—specifically, the need for more from more people.

As organizations began to greatly expand in size, reach, and complexity 150 years ago, management experienced an explosion of sorts, evolving from an intuitive, simple process into a sophisticated job now held by many millions of people worldwide. In a somewhat similar way, as the context around us is becoming more multifaceted and speeding up in terms of change, creating a greater need for faster movement and agility inside enterprises, leadership has begun undergoing a revolution of sorts.

We speak of a revolution in what it means to lead but even more so in regard to who and how many people need to provide that leadership to create winning organizations and a prospering society for all.

Management Is Not Leadership

Too often, "leadership" and "management" are still thought of as positional (though the research on this point says it is not). Within the framework of the more-than-century-old modern organization, that means a few people at the top of the hierarchy provide leadership and a much larger group in the middle of the hierarchy provide management. There is much truth there, which is why this concept persists. But the reality of organizations that flourish in a rapidly changing world looks increasingly different.

Leadership is about establishing a direction and vision for the future, aligning people around that vision, and then motivating and inspiring them to take action. Leadership mobilizes people to overcome significant barriers, create difficult change, and, in extreme cases, achieve truly astonishing results. All this is to be contrasted with management, which might be usefully defined as the set of structures and policies and actions that enable systems of people and technology to operate reliably and efficiently, despite size, geographical reach, or other sorts of sometimes great complexity.

Unfortunately, one of the reasons businesses, governments, and other entities struggle is because of confusion about the purposes of, and differences between, management and leadership. Management is often called leadership, especially when it is driven by people near the top of a hierarchy. Most modern organizations throw up many barriers to leadership at lower levels, and when it does somehow emerge it is usually labeled something else: initiative, good management, or high potential.

But the reality of what leadership is in terms of behavior and what it accomplishes is clear if one reads enough biographies of people whom historians universally describe as great leaders. In their actions, you find a clear pattern: these men and women either lived in tumultuous times and were central figures in motivating and inspiring others to adapt and win, or they actually created tumultuous times themselves with a vision of a better future, and then motivated or inspired others to adapt to achieve the vision and prosper greatly. In either case, the changes associated with them are so significant, and the outcomes so positive, that they are remembered centuries after their deaths.

These stories can be breathtaking. In the social sphere, one finds Nelson Mandela becoming president in a country filled with hate and fear. Study his actions and we find a highly visible beacon of hope, joy, and determination to grasp the opportunity to start building a modern, black-led and governed South Africa. This positive emotional attitude, almost totally missing before his election, grew and grew, replacing both anger and anxiety.

Mandela took hundreds of actions, some large like the "Truth and Reconciliation Commission," some seemingly small or marginal, like developing a friendship with the white captain of the country's rugby team, and some on the surface simply odd, like his lunches with the widows of former apartheid leaders. But inherent in so much of what he did was calming the overheated Survive in the country's population, and possibly in himself, and beginning to activate real Thrive. So much of what he did created urgency around joint opportunity, a growing diverse coalition driving the work, a vision of a whole new nation, communication for broad-based buy-in, the empowerment of more people, and the planning for, accomplishment of, and celebrating of wins.

As a result, people of all races were mobilized to build, not destroy. What many experts predicted would inevitably turn into a horrific civil war, with enormous loss of life, did not happen. People took a different path, still very challenging today, but *infinitely* better than many people were predicting.

Mandela's story is usually told as an example of the possibilities with a larger-than-life leader. But for our purposes there is an even richer story here. Through an intuitive understanding of human nature, leadership, and the social/organizational barriers to change, Mandela inspired a group to lift itself up and lead itself away from what many saw as an inevitable crash landing. The result was amazing positive change, under incredibly challenging circumstances, in a remarkably short period of time, with shockingly superior results.

In the business sphere, one of the great stories of the twentieth century has at its center a person with a very different personality than Mandela's, yet with a leadership dynamic that was much the same. Thomas Watson took three small, unknown businesses and helped people build the first truly global high-tech firm, IBM. He did so in part, again, through a focus on opportunity, creating highly positive, inspirational emotions associated with pride in winning, camaraderie, and, increasingly over time, a belief that employees were working for something special. The truly special included helping customers, helping the government in WWII, helping create educational opportunities, and helping build a firm where people were actually encouraged to *think*.

The contrast between Watson's way of operating and that of most other businesses was especially visible during the Depression. During this difficult time, companies shrank. Layoffs, sometimes very large, were the norm. With Survive so often overheated, innovation largely disappeared. Watson, unlike almost all of his peers, pursued a strategy of keeping his workers busy producing new machines, even when demand was slack. He was among those whose strategy pioneered employee relation practices, IBM being among the first corporations to provide group life insurance (1934), survivor benefits (1935), and paid vacations (1937). When many companies were largely ignoring true innovation, IBM's strategy supported the building of one of the finest R&D labs in the world in Endicott, New York, in 1933.

When the Roosevelt administration passed the Social Security Act in 1935, the government solicited bids to maintain the employment records for 26 million people. With creative products, a large inventory ready to ship, and a skilled and dedicated workforce, IBM won the huge contract easily.

In a time when so many firms went out of business, IBM grew during the Depression: in sales, profits, employment, and reputation. And the lessons in this story are as relevant today as they were nearly a century ago. The same dynamic of finding ways to invest and look for opportunities in a crisis is playing out as we write this for some companies because of the COVID-19 pandemic.

The Waiting-for-Lincoln Trap

The study of larger-than-life figures such as Mandela and Watson provides insights that can be very beneficial as we try to deal with today's reality. But such research can also mislead in a very fundamental and dangerous way. The implicit message, even when historians do not explicitly make the argument, is that the key (and really the only key) to dealing with a rapidly shifting context is that rare, heroic, intuitively brilliant, brave king, queen, president, prime minister, general, or CEO. It's all about Lincoln, Mandela, Victoria, and their extremely rare peers.

This conclusion has *some* important truth to it—but it's far from the whole story. Although not everyone who seriously studies great figures would agree, we think it is very clear that if there were no Churchill, Martin Luther King, Jr., or Thomas Watson, the world would have evolved differently in some important ways. So the point is not that such people are inconsequential media figureheads, or had they not existed someone else would have played the same role, and just as brilliantly. Quite the contrary. *The point is that we cannot depend upon mass-producing heroic figures to solve humanity's problems. There must be another way.*

And there is.

The solution, as shown in the stories in this book, is for many, many more people, regardless of where they sit in an organization or community, to step up and lead.

Dramatic Expansion of Leadership in Action

Faced with increasing global demand, a medical products company launched a grassroots movement to change the way it worked, and focused on an opportunity that emphasized building a quality mindset across the organization. They recognized that deficiencies in quality meant less product reaching patients and saving lives.

In 2015, they launched a transformation effort following most of the principles outlined in this book. They began by pulling together a diverse team of employees, from all levels of the organization (from shop floor to senior leaders) who were passionate about the opportunity.

Luis, a third-shift production line worker, applied to be on the team. His natural leadership, emotional intelligence, and motivation were immediately evident to others. As a volunteer, Luis became an incredible advocate for the movement. He had one-on-one conversations with dozens of colleagues, and many more collective encounters, recruiting sometimes up to 60 new shop-floor volunteers per week. Speaking as a peer, he was able to calm some of the natural Survive activation this work initially sparked for many shop floor workers (e.g. feeling their jobs were now being hyper-scrutinized, without the necessary support from managers). He was also able to help activate Thrive by giving them a voice and a role in the transformation.

For example, Luis gathered 92 of his shop floor colleagues to brainstorm possible improvements. They generated 269 proposals that ranged from changes to the visual boards to manage work, to ideas that would individually save hundreds of thousands of dollars and improve production output.

Perhaps his biggest impact was the renewed belief among employees in the organization's purpose and management capability. The leadership role Luis played in making this happen is probably best summed up by a quote from one of the managers from his facility:

> Luis' energy brightens up a room, and his enthusiasm for changing the way that we work is contagious. When we first met Lou, we had yet to connect with shop floor employees in his department, but his passion for our movement would soon provide the bridge that we were looking for. As we sit on a global engagement team, we often talk about how to engage shop floor employees, and we are all in agreement that each site should focus on finding their "Luis" or "Luises." For our site, we are just extremely grateful that he found us.

This type of leadership is invaluable, not only because it creates bridges within the organization (between management and shop floor employees, silos, regions, etc.), but also because it motivates and inspires other unusual suspects to step up and contribute to achieving their organization's opportunities in new ways.

We have seen many stories of unexpected individuals making dramatic impacts, stories like the union worker at an energy company who was able to drastically increase engagement by translating the company's transformational opportunity to the front lines. He single-handedly got in front of more than 1,000 people to talk about their biggest opportunity, how it tied to the company's strategy, and how new ways of working would make their jobs (and lives) better. He helped employees connect their day-to-day work to the company's transformation effort, encouraged them to take action on countless improvements big and small, and bridged a gap between union and non-union employees, which had never really been done before.

Or the employee who had previously been struggling, who was instrumental in translating a leader's business challenge into a massive opportunity. She guided a team to make changes that saved 20 million dollars annually, improved customer satisfaction, and in the process reignited her passion for her work. The latter changed the trajectory of her career and those of many more who were part of the effort.

Or the night shift worker who helped increase output on a constrained production line by 15% through the simplest of solutions, one that the engineers would never have thought of. The improvement was possible because of an insight that the employee gained from his 20 years of operating the line.

All of these people stepped up to lead in various ways, despite not having positional leadership. In doing so, they helped accelerate their organizations' achievement of critical and inspiring possibilities. All gained a personal sense of accomplishment that was deeply meaningful. And many of them won employee awards and/or received promotions for the first time in their careers.

Creating the Right Environment and Culture

Some readers will wonder if these sorts of leadership-from-below stories are inevitably rare because modern management-driven structures tend to shut down leadership even in middle levels, never mind at the bottom of the hierarchy.

This observation about the barriers to more leadership in modern organizations is accurate, and in many organizations, unless you are at the top of the hierarchy, demonstrating leadership behaviors takes courage and may be unnatural. But there *is* a solution that encourages and supports more of this behavior. We have already discussed it in earlier chapters.

This solution helps create an environment that allows for and promotes leadership from everywhere. It involves molding modern organizations to fit an age of exceptionally complex and rapid change. That means not eliminating all the good this relatively new invention of management can do, but adding to it. Specifically, we mean adding an organic, dynamic network structure—sitting alongside the traditional hierarchy. This dual system is similar to what virtually all successful organizations have, at some point, relatively early in their histories. At that stage one finds a balance between an agile, adaptive, entrepreneurial way of working, similar to a start-up, and more reliable, efficient processes to keep the day-to-day on track, similar to what we usually find in mature enterprises.

A dual system, operating well, can support a diverse many, who want to help with change (in ways beyond their job description) and have their hearts deeply attached to a compelling opportunity. It can support people in all departments and levels who want to help provide the leadership needed to create a sense of urgency, develop and act on needed strategic initiatives, mobilize volunteers, overcome barriers, have and celebrate successes, keep momentum building, and actually make and sustain change again and again. This dual operating system can make leadership as a behavior seem more natural and acceptable anywhere.

We have written elsewhere how some organizations have created dual systems step-by-step, and the greater leadership that results (see Notes). Here we would add one additional point, which has to do with the role that culture can play.

Starting with the research described in Chapter 6 on creating cultures that help you adapt, and in many subsequent efforts, we have consistently seen the importance of culture in enabling the kind of leadership everywhere that is essential for today's context of faster and more complex change.

Specifically, companies with cultures that equally value all stakeholders, and are thus more focused on changes in the product markets, the labor markets, financial markets, and relevant communities are far more likely to encourage leadership and engagement from all levels. Within such cultures, people recognize that the only way to keep up with the increasing flow of relevant information is to tap into the insights and ideas of all of one's staff, not only those designated as leaders or managers, or the small group of "go-to" employees.

The leaders at the top of the hierarchy in these organizations then quite *logically* value leadership from everyone. Through role modeling, recognition, rewards, and even accountability, they reinforce a culture that is conducive to more leadership from anywhere. Relatively simple and clear cultural values and principles, as opposed to complex (and sometimes inconsistent) formal rules and policies, help employees know what is truly expected. This calms Survive (for example, by removing the fear of stepping out of line) and can also activate Thrive by providing room for taking initiative within broad guidelines.

Bottom line: Organizations that operate with a dual system are able to reduce the barriers to the kind of leadership from anywhere and everywhere highlighted by the story of Luis and others earlier in this chapter. And enterprises with adaptive cultures are more likely to make what is generally not found today—leadership from many sources—even more possible.

Tactics for Calming Overheated Survive and Activating Dormant Thrive

Whether within a system and culture that is already primed for it or not, creating more leadership also ultimately requires appropriate activation of Survive and Thrive Channels. With its opportunity focus, positive emotional orientation, inclination to think broadly, and bias toward action to capitalize on opportunity, Thrive hardwiring is closely connected to leadership. And with too much Survive easily shutting down Thrive, an overabundance of Survive is typically associated with a lack of leadership.

Numerous researchers have written extensively about how individuals can more effectively calm Survive and activate Thrive for themselves. It is outside the scope of this book to summarize all of that thinking here. In the following sections, we include some high-level strategies for managing your individual Survive and Thrive—with an emphasis on those actions that better enable leaders to help *organizations* optimize their Survive/Thrive activation. (For readers who want to dig deeper into strategies for individuals, we have provided a number of references in the Notes, mostly from well-regarded thought leaders in positive psychology.)

For many reasons, what we generally find today are organizations that have an overactive Survive and an underactive Thrive.

So, what can you do?

Taking Stock

Any attempt to address this imbalance must start with taking stock of the current situation. As a leader, it's helpful to do this for yourself first, so you can manage how you show up for those you are leading. This often means reflecting on and identifying one's own Survive and Thrive triggers, as well as assessing the current level of activation on both channels.

While the Survive/Thrive system is hardwired in our bodies, the sensitivity and response to different triggers is informed by our past experiences and contexts. For example, shifting roles within an organization may trigger a significant Survive response in one individual but not at all in another. What's more, after a few successful career transitions, even the individual who had an intense Survive response the first time may not be triggered at all. An understanding of your own triggers in a particular situation generally requires a deliberate, thoughtful assessment of your reactions and feelings—and how these affect your behavior as a leader.

Similarly, at an organizational level, it is also useful to assess the current state. Is there a lot of anxiety across the organization or are people excited and anticipating the future? Does this vary across different departments? What seems to trigger overheated Survive responses in general as well as in specific departments, silos, areas? Context and history matter, such as a company's past success or lack thereof with integrating new digital tools. Processes and systems can prime the Survive radar by making it less or more sensitive. We will discuss this in more detail later in the chapter.

Priming Yourself to Lead: Activating Your Personal Thrive and Mitigating Survive

In order to demonstrate leadership and inspire leadership from others, it is imperative that your own Survive is activated (but not overactivated) *and* your Thrive is activated (not underactivated).

If your Thrive is not adequately engaged, you can trigger it by reflecting on opportunities that are both real and personally exciting or meaningful (or both). Focusing on the opportunities to learn and develop and thinking concretely about the role you can play will also help activate Thrive. It can help to ask yourself questions like: What will a positive outcome look like? How will I feel about that outcome? What changes do I personally feel invested in contributing to? What are the most interesting or exciting activities ahead of us?

If activating your Thrive is difficult because Survive is overheated, you start by recognizing and naming your Survive triggers. You can look for ways to take a breath and calm down, which for most of us is much easier said than done. You work on learning to identify when you are having an overwrought Survive response. This knowledge can help break a cycle of negative thinking.

Managing your own Survive and Thrive activation allows you to better recognize threats, ignore noise that is not about real crises, role model authentic excitement (and build that same authentic excitement in others), and begin to take useful/needed action on the opportunities ahead of you and the organization.

Activating Thrive and Modulating Survive in an Organization

In an organizational context, aggressively activating Thrive starts with filling the organization with a lot more thinking, talking, and discussion of opportunities, not just problems. Relentlessly finding opportunities, even in the midst of challenges, crises, or pandemics, requires understanding the landscape. What are the challenges in front of the organization and what is possible if it innovates and thinks differently? What customer, employee, community, supplier, or shareholder needs is it not addressing, and what is the payoff if it does?

With answers to these questions, leadership from you means flooding your organization with communication about the possible opportunities. This is communication that touches hearts, not just minds, and that leads people to *want to engage*, not just *have to* do their jobs.

There will be some individuals who are ready to take action immediately—and good leaders capitalize on that energy. Rather than overinvesting in getting resisters on board, they start where the energy is and let momentum build from there. And they don't limit themselves to giving space to the same people they always lean on. Rather, they encourage leadership actions from anyone, including those who may not have been seen as the traditional high performers.

Leaders also recognize that articulating the rationale behind an opportunity and removing obvious barriers to action is not enough. They activate Thrive by increasing, sometimes very significantly, how often people feel what most of us would call positive emotions associated with seizing and capitalizing on organizationally relevant opportunities—feeling excited, happy, filled with pride and purpose, passionate, a sense of camaraderie, even joy. Opportunity, as a purely intellectual concept, is not what triggers Thrive, nor is it what Thrive, once started, naturally induces. Leaders help their teams take actions to connect personally with the opportunity, take a learning perspective, and clarify their role in achieving the opportunity.

Aggressively activating Thrive Channels is impossible in a modern organizational setting without vastly increasing the emphasis on and the discussion of opportunities. And all the evidence we have says that "vastly" is not an overstatement, especially in older and bigger bureaucratic organizations.

A massive increase is needed because *so little* of the current conversation outside of fast-moving and young entrepreneurial settings is about opportunity. Deeply embedded ways of working get in the way, easily overwhelming the reality of new opportunities. Even when a need for change is recognized, most often this need is framed as a threat, a burning platform. This fear-driven motivation encourages some initial action, but it also can easily shut down Thrive and with it the creativity and innovation that could result in real solutions. Stepping up to lead without formal authority always takes courage and the greater the general level of fear and anxiety in the organization, the harder it is for individuals to take the interpersonal risk to do so.

Reducing Survive-Inducing Noise in an Enterprise

At the heart of it, the modern organization is about removing uncertainty and minimizing risk, which leads to a focus on threats, or perceived threats, which can easily be any actions that challenge the status quo.

We have all seen these sometimes subtle messages:

- Break one of the seemingly endless real or imagined policies and get into who knows how much trouble.

- Don't do exactly what the boss, or the boss's boss, or anyone higher in the hierarchy wants and face small or very large sanctions.

- Miss this metric for sales, inventory control, cash flow, budget limits, and so on and face potentially serious consequences.

- Be late for meetings, don't dress appropriately, or violate anything in the culture and watch out.

While a healthy level of Survive activation is necessary to spot and tackle real threats, this constant barrage of anxiety overactivates Survive and shuts down Thrive. Mitigating Survive requires identifying Survive-activating triggers, including management processes, metrics, and expectations that send messages like the ones above.

The sheer volume of activity in modern organizations is another reason that makes it difficult for individuals to lead and take action against the most important opportunities. Many organizations and their employees are overwhelmed with initiatives, projects, meetings, spreadsheets to be studied, and emails to be answered. A question we often hear nowadays from CEOs, executives, middle managers, and still others is: What should I stop doing, and where should I focus my time?

Looking at this question through the lens of the Survive/Thrive system provides a useful answer. Given the strength of the Survive Channel, our default is to focus on threats *over* opportunities. This new way of thinking suggests that prioritizing what to focus on logically starts with evaluating the *real* threats *and* opportunities, and then clarifying where a Survive-driven response is needed and where Thrive activation is necessary.

With this in mind, you evaluate actions and initiatives through both their effectiveness at addressing a problem and their capacity to activate Survive. It means asking: Could this action trigger a Survive response in the organization? If so, proceed only if you are convinced that it is addressing a true threat of some magnitude. In addition, transparency about why the action is being taken and the outcomes you anticipate can provide context and prevent unfounded fear and anxiety. The risk mitigation focus of modern organizations tends not to consider the role played by strategies that create more oversight and control—like new quality metrics or increased supervision of expenditures—in increasing workforce anxiety and fear and hence contributing to overheated Survive.

For the most important opportunities, you continue to use the Survive/Thrive lens to, for example, reimagine outdated metrics that inadvertently send messages counter to the opportunity. You can shape communications to lead more often with talk of opportunity. You do so not only with employees and peers and bosses, but sometimes with customers and investors. You celebrate behaviors that move the organization toward capitalizing on the opportunities, not just short-term financial outcomes.

Even with talented top management, big organizations can inadvertently trigger anxiety because of their size and the accompanying bureaucracy. What can often look from the executive conference room like a lot of emphasis on opportunity becomes in fact a very small force that is overwhelmed by noise screaming from an overwrought Survive Channel.

What starts out as an inspiring call to action, to innovate and capture opportunities in a changing marketplace, can even be just another Survive-inducing set of anxiety triggers by the time it is translated into targets, goals, budgets, and dashboards. And one more report given to management about a strategic plan, or one more speech at the annual management meeting about vision, does little to change this. More pressure—holding people "accountable" for executing plans based on an analysis of opportunities—often does nothing except *increase* activity driven by the Survive side. The Thrive Channel, and the corresponding innovation and opportunity seeking, remains underactivated.

This challenge of translating the inspiring opportunity throughout the organization is exacerbated by the "middle management" problem. Launched from the top, a complex change process seems to run into more resistance two or three levels down than at the front lines of an enterprise. Frustrated individuals refer to the "rock in the middle" or use even less-flattering terms. These upper- to middle-level managers may sometimes even be demonized.

But what if these managers are not any different than those above or below them (except perhaps for years of experience or potential to take on greater responsibilities)? What if they are simply in a perpetual state of Survive-agitation created by too much "noise"—from management systems, bosses, and external pressures that seem to scream "problem here, problem there" on a daily basis. And what about the noise brought by metrics that introduce an ongoing stream of bad news, or barriers created by lawyers, quality staff, or HR compliance people? What if these managers are also caught in the middle of silo politics, or competing demands from above and below? What if their bosses often end meetings with comments only about the downside consequences of problems or speeches about burning platforms?

We have seen that the middle management "problem" can be greatly mitigated or even eliminated through a better understanding of the unique context and triggers to which Survive Channels are responding. Ultimately, the only solution is to calm Survive and amplify a much louder, consistent voice that can awaken the Thrive radar—which is one thing that exceptional leaders always do, no matter where they are in an enterprise.

Fueling Thrive in an Organization by Celebrating Progress

The focus on opportunity and envisioning a better future can light up the Thrive Channel. With a steady dose of positive emotions and the corresponding chemicals, this activation can continue for a remarkably long period of time.

The role that repeated positive emotion plays is easy to see in virtually all the great leadership stories from the twentieth century.

Again and again one finds in those stories not just an intellectually and emotionally compelling opportunity but also actions and behaviors that continue to align purpose, keep focus on an exciting future, and elicit positive emotions. Despite barriers, people are initially mobilized to build with speed something of significance that takes a group into a better future. Success is celebrated with every win. With each success, people's energy is reinvigorated and more people are inclined to want to join the movement.

ENCOURAGE MORE LEADERSHIP FROM MORE PEOPLE: CALM OVERHEATED SURVIVE + ACTIVATE DORMANT THRIVE

TAKE STOCK TO IDENTIFY BARRIERS TO MORE LEADERSHIP

Name your personal Survive and Thrive triggers; assess your own current level of activation. Consider the organization's current state and most common triggers.

ACTIVATE THRIVE + MITIGATE SURVIVE FOR YOURSELF

Find personal purpose, meaning, and opportunity. Recognize when your personal triggers are happening and find ways to stop the negative cycle.

ACTIVATE THRIVE + MODULATE SURVIVE IN AN ORGANIZATION

Drastically increase the communication and emphasis on opportunities. Go where the energy is, and unleash the power of engaged, passionate employees—from everyone in the organization.

REDUCE SURVIVE-INDUCING NOISE

Cut out messages, processes and systems that inadvertently trigger Survive and take away from the opportunity. Give yourself (and others) permission to say no, and to stop non-value-add activity.

FUEL THE THRIVE CHANNEL—CELEBRATE PROGRESS

Don't wait for the big "win" at the end—acknowledge and celebrate along the way. Continue to foster the positive emotions created by an active Thrive.

The keys are to maintain an unwavering focus on opportunity, engage as many others as possible to help with the change tasks, give them permission and air cover to take action, keep the noise level down, and celebrate successes along the way.

When you do all this well, be prepared for those hard-to-imagine results. They are needed. They will come.

Chapter 11

The New Normal

As we wrote this book, the COVID-19 pandemic was spreading across the world with an almost incomprehensible effect on hundreds of millions if not billions of lives. For the first time in at least the last fifty years, we faced a crisis that reached all parts of the globe and directly impacted people in every country.

In most cases, this situation was viewed as episodic, something that needed to be weathered before returning to the pre-crisis levels of change, uncertainty, and disruption. This belief was highlighted to us in an inquiry posed by the leader of the U.S. operations of a European company. "I have a question," she asked. "COVID has actually helped force us to find some new practices that are better than those we employed before the pandemic. I don't want to lose those new practices when COVID-19 is over. So what can we do?"

Implicit in her question is the idea that we can usefully think of this time in three phases: before COVID-19, during the pandemic, and post-COVID-19, when things could settle back into a somewhat better "new normal." While this is a valid viewpoint, particularly in regard to preserving the positive changes that COVID-19 has thrust upon us, there is a more important lesson to be taken from the crisis.

Lessons from the Crisis

The lesson from the current pandemic, and the high levels of uncertainty we are all feeling as individuals and organizations, is that *increased rapid and complex change is becoming the new normal*. While what we are experiencing today may feel like a galactic shift that will last a year or so but will then go back to some variation of a steady state, the current crisis is actually just an extreme example of the increasing level of uncertainty that we were already experiencing. The uncertainty index that we presented in the introduction of this book clearly shows a sharp upward trend well before COVID-19 ever infected a single human being.

Zoom out, and you can see that this uncertainty, speed, and volatility is the continuation of a development that has, to a limited degree, been going on for at least 15,000 years, to a larger degree for 150 to 200 years, and unambiguously for the last 4 decades. It is driven most of all by evolving (and sometimes now exploding) technologies and geographic integration. In the chapter on digital transformations, we saw how quickly the Information Age is evolving even compared to the Industrial Age. In addition to the pace, the qualitative nature of the change is also more encompassing, touching both our professional and our personal lives. The restrictions on movement and in-person interactions forced on us by the pandemic have served to highlight and accelerate the digitalization of our lives.

It is not possible to predict exactly how this will manifest itself in terms of economic, health, political, and other issues in 50, 5, or even 1 year. While experts often trace causality once an event has transpired, predicting how future events will play out is much more difficult. The 2008 financial crisis, the fall of the Soviet Union, or the Arab Spring all seemed inevitable in hindsight, but not many people predicted them ahead of time.

What we can predict, based especially on the evidence of the last few hundred years, is that we will continue to see more unanticipated events that include threats (and sometimes huge threats) and opportunities (and sometimes huge opportunities). With the growing interconnectedness of the world today, we can also be sure that these events will increasingly have direct and indirect impacts across the globe, not limited to just one country or one region.

The mismatch between the reality of more change as the new normal and our inclination as human beings and organizations to look for stability has tremendous implications—perhaps most fundamentally that we need to further develop and use the emerging science of change or we risk peril. The good news is that this science and the new methods it gives us for strategic planning, digital transformation, restructuring, and more is actionable, teachable, and has been already shown to produce results that can seem astounding.

Using the Understanding of Human Nature to Handle Growing Uncertainty and Complexity

The advancements of human society over the last few hundred years have resulted in much of the world's population no longer facing literal survival triggers on a frequent basis. However, this development has created even more threats to our status, ego, and reputations that, to our hardwiring, are often indistinguishable from physical attacks. The evolutionary mechanism meant to aid our survival by putting us on high alert in truly threatening situations is in today's world causing almost constant anxiety for many people. Falling stock prices, racial tensions, images of hurricanes and forest fires, and deadly viruses are all perceived as agonizing *personal* threats.

In this sort of environment, we will undoubtedly face the risk, quite possibly growing, of noise overstimulating the Survive Channel, which in turn shuts down or dampens the Thrive Channel. This is particularly troublesome at a time when we require a *more* activated Thrive to create the mental/emotional conditions necessary for the curiosity and innovation we need to deal with, and take advantage of, the context in which we live.

The situation is far from hopeless, and the potential negative outcomes are not inevitable. *The science of the brain's hardwiring gives us many insights on how to avoid this problem and seize the opportunities that more change brings us.* We certainly have enough stories, some summarized in this book, to show the incredible possibilities when the Survive/Thrive system is appropriately engaged, as well as how people have done just that. While our focus has been the organization, many of the lessons apply to how we as individuals can start to drive lasting and beneficial change in our personal and professional lives.

Reconstructing the Modern Organization

As we have seen, the modern organization can in many cases be an anchor on accelerated, sensible, and needed change. A few forward-looking leaders and entrepreneurs, mostly at young technology companies, have recognized that the fundamental design of the modern organizations is unsuited to today's need for speed and agility. These companies are starting to experiment with new organizational structures and new operating systems.

For these companies, particularly early in their lifecycles, the risk aversion, incremental change, and lack of innovation that is too often a byproduct of formal processes and systems is antithetical to their entrepreneurial spirit. The command-and-control structure of formal hierarchies does not fit with their values or the realities of running a rapidly growing company. However, what is also increasingly clear is that a wholesale rejection of the modern organizational system is not the right solution to this problem. With scale and organizational complexity comes the need for robust and reliable management practices. *The answer, as we discussed in earlier chapters, is an organizational structure and operating system that is built upon both a robust hierarchy and a changing, evolving network.*

The vast majority of people today have never seen the dual operating systems, or the adaptive cultures, that can transform modern organizations into more agile race cars and do so without sacrificing the reliability and consistency of a family sedan.

In the coming new normal, it is a very good bet that the typical form of organizations will change. The big question is: how quickly and how proactively?

Engineering More Leadership from More People to Drive Needed Change

It is also a relatively safe bet that the increasing need for collaboration and teaming in organizations will lead to more and more people providing nontrivial leadership that makes a difference. Roles and job functions have gotten more specialized and the need for integration has accelerated. It is no longer possible for a few leaders at the top of the organization to have all the required information or skills to make good decisions about the diverse activities within a twenty first century dynamic marketplace.

Operationally, this means more people actively looking for meaningful changes in the marketplace, relevant technologies, the financial situation, labor markets, and more; more people helping to create a broad sense of urgency to deal with threats and opportunities; more working with others in coalitions to guide change; more helping to clarify direction and develop strategic initiatives, big and small, for moving in selected directions;

more helping with the vast communication challenge in a rapidly shifting, volatile world; more stepping forward to volunteer to go beyond their jobs in a narrow sense and removing barriers so others can too; more new and better results from these efforts in shorter periods of time to create credibility and momentum; more people helping to overcome the forces that lean toward declaring victory too soon; and more seeing the need for, and the methods our emerging theory of change give us, to sustain new ways of operating once achieved.

Operationally, this also means more people embracing the principles, from the emerging science of leading change, that have been used in all the remarkable stories told in this book: the need to draw on not just the select few but the diverse many; the need to go beyond have-to motivation in drawing people in and include want-to; the power of engaging not just the head but the heart; the necessity of operating not just through formal hierarchy and management but more informal networks and leadership.

At the more senior levels in management, *one of the most important tasks will increasingly be creating the conditions that encourage leadership from everywhere*. The shift in the role of employees within organizations has already started in many contexts and settings. The flatter hierarchy in most Silicon Valley firms, for example, encourages more people to see providing direction, initiative, and leadership as part of their role.

A lot has been written about the expectations of the new generation of workers. What is clear is that for many Millennials the idea of leadership is quite different than previous generations. The role models for business leaders from the last two decades lean more heavily toward inclusion, curiosity, and flexibility than confidence, infallibility, and imposing charisma. This bodes well for the kind of dispersed leadership that will be needed to build organizations that can move fast and pivot quickly.

Another reason to feel encouraged about the development of more leadership is that technological tools, when used appropriately, can be great enablers for individuals to step up in various ways and contribute to leading successful change.

How much will happen here, how quickly, and how uniformly across sectors and regions? Again, that is hard to predict, except to say that *the early movers, who use the science of change and the playbooks created for its practical application, will develop a significant competitive advantage.*

Back to the Issue of Stakes

Even for mid-sized enterprises, any single organization's success or failure at coming to grips with our increasingly volatile and fast-changing world could affect the lives of many, many thousands of people. We include employees, obviously, but also executives, customers, shareholders, suppliers, and communities. The gap between what is possible on the high end and what is possible on the low end has been growing for decades, and that will surely continue, at least for a while. For a single large organization, and there are thousands of them globally, the number of people who could be touched in an incredibly positive or disturbingly negative way is in the tens or hundreds of millions.

One does not need to project out 50 or 100 years to see large differences in outcomes depending upon the choices we make. For an individual company, in five years the difference between handling change exceptionally well versus poorly could mean billions in wealth created or squandered, thousands of jobs created or lost, and dozens of products or services that are highly valued or irrelevant to tens of thousands or millions of customers. In less than five years, mistakes could close a big plant in a small town and cause havoc for everyone who lives there. Smart choices in one or two years could mean the difference between a managerial and frontline workforce that finds life wonderfully meaningful versus an agonizing source of constant stress that affects their health. And for the head of an organization, the right path over five years could mean retiring with a legacy to be deeply proud of for the rest of one's life. Or the opposite.

Beyond single organizations, our collective capacity and ability as a global village to deal with rapid, complex change will certainly be tested in the coming decades. Whether combating a changing climate, resolving the disruption of labor markets from changing technology and artificial intelligence, navigating financial crises, or rethinking how we work and live in the face of global pandemics and other public health threats, how we come to grips with even more change will have consequences that are very hard to conceive.

It does not always seem like it, but on average the lives of humans across the planet have been changing for the better for centuries now. Statistics on life expectancy, infant mortality, and violent deaths certainly bear this out. This book is meant to inspire people with the idea that by taking action in new ways, not only can we respond to rapid change but we can accelerate this rate of progress. We also hope that you will think about leadership differently: not as the responsibility of a few unique, charismatic individuals, but rather as a set of behaviors we can all exhibit in some ways.

In Chapter 1, we said our aspiration was that this book would inspire you to get-after-it. In conclusion, we sincerely, urgently, and passionately hope you do just that.

Notes

For the reader who would like to explore in more depth some of the research, history, or stories mentioned in the book, we include these notes.

Preface

The list of books that make up the bulk of the research program described in the preface can be found in the "bookshelf" section of www.kotterinc.com/research-and-perspectives.

Chapter 1: Threats and Opportunities in a Rapidly Changing World

Data showing how so many powerful forces are changing faster and faster can be found in many places. A reader interested in what this generally looks like can go to the graphs in Chapter 1 in John Kotter's *Accelerate* (Boston: Harvard Business School Publishing, 2014).

Chapter 2: The Emerging Science of Change

If you are interested in learning more about the basis for the conceptualization of the Survive/Thrive system, the description of the two states of neurological and hormonal functioning can be found in research by Hazy and

Boyatzis, "Emotional contagion and proto-organizing in human interaction dynamics," *Frontiers in Psychology* (2015) 6:806

For a very readable summary of the neuroscience behind the ideas, see Appendix 1 in Robert Sapolosky's excellent book *Behave* (London: Penguin Random House UK, 2018).

The Drucker reference was to his seminal study of General Motors: *The Concept of the Corporation* (New York: John Day Company, 1946).

Our take on the emergence of the modern organization has been heavily aided by the Pulitzer Prize–winning business historian Al Chandler. See, for example, *The Visible Hand: The Managerial Revolution in American Business* (Cambridge, Mass.: Belknap Press, 1977).

Early examples of the research stream on purposeful organizational change efforts include *Management and the Worker* by Fritz Roethlisberger and W.J. Dickson (Cambridge, Mass: Harvard University Press, 1939), a study of Western Electric Company's Hawthorne Works in Chicago, and *The Changing of Organizational Behavior Patterns* by Paul Lawrence (Cambridge, Mass.: Harvard University press, 1958), a study of the Stop & Shop Supermarket companies.

Our research on why transformations fail was reported in detail in John Kotter's book, *Leading Change* (Boston: Harvard Business Review Press, 1996).

Readers not familiar with the name Matsushita can learn about this extraordinary businessman who created the firm Panasonic (and much more) in John Kotter's *Matsushita Leadership* (New York: Free Press, 1998).

The dual operating system is discussed in the book, *Accelerate: Building Strategic Agility for a Faster-Moving World* (Boston: Harvard Business School Publishing, 2014).

Chapter 3: "Strategic Planning" That Delivers *Results*

The quote from the BCG consultant is from Walter Kiechel's *The Lords of Strategy* (Boston: Harvard Business Review Press, 2010).

For more on the original thinking and development of strategy, see Michael Porter's *Competitive Strategy* (New York: Free Press, 1980) and Bruce D. Henderson's *On Corporate Strategy* (New York: Harper Collins, 1979).

Details on the study of 100 big change efforts that showed that the key to the most successful efforts was not sophisticated data and analytics can be found in John Kotter and Dan Cohen's book, *The Heart of Change* (Boston: Harvard Business Review Press, 2012).

Chapter 4: Digital Transformation That Is Truly Transformational

For additional reading on the common pitfalls of digital transformation, there are many useful *Harvard Business Review* articles, including "Why So Many High-Profile Digital Transformations Fail" (March 2018) by Thomas H. Davenport and George Westerman; "The Two Big Reasons That Digital Transformations Fail" (October 2019) by Mike Sutcliff, Raghav Narsalay, and Aarohi Sen; and "Discovery-Driven Digital Transformation" (May–June 2020) by Rite Gunther McGrath and Ryan McManus.

For more on Best Buy's digital transformation, see their November 2012 investor presentation at https://corporate.bestbuy.com/wp-content/uploads/BestBuy_Web_FINAL.pdf.

To read more about GE's digital transformation, see the 2019 IMD case study, prepared by Lisa Duke under the supervision of Stéphane J.G. Girod, "Digital Transformation at GE: Shifting Minds for Agility."

For more on "The Problem with Data," see John Kotter's whitepaper on the subject at kotterinc.com/research-and-perspectives/the-problem-with-data/.

For another interesting perspective on the downside of big data, see Cathy O'Neil's book *Weapons of Math Destruction: How Big Data Increases Inequality and Threatens Democracy* (New York: Crown Publishers, 2016).

Chapter 5: Restructuring Without Killing Innovation and Your Future

The story of the Kraft Heinz merger, its bid for Unilever, and the dramatic fall in the stock price has been reported extensively. One good summary is a piece by Julie Creswell and David Yaffe-Bellany, "When Mac & Cheese and Ketchup Don't Mix," *New York Times*, September 24, 2019. For an analysis on the failure, see John Kotter and Gaurav Gupta, "The Missing Ingredient in Kraft-Heinz's Restructuring," *Harvard Business Review Online*, September 26, 2019.

For more information on the studies that provided the statistics regarding layoffs, see Art Budros, "The New Capitalism and Organizational Rationality: The Adoption of Downsizing Programs, 1979–1994," *Social Forces* (No 1, 1997) 76: 229–249, and from the McKinsey Global Institute, "An Economy That Works: Job Creating and America's Future," June 2011.

For more information on the S&P Capital IQ and Bruce Henderson Institute analysis, see Reeves et al., "The Truth about Corporate Transformation," *MIT Sloan Management Review*, January 31, 2018, http://mitsmr.com/2DQSmF4.

Chapter 6: Cultural Change That Helps You Adapt

For a great recent history of cultural anthropology and the adventurous scientists who pioneered it, see Charles King's *Gods of the Upper Air: How a Circle of Renegade Anthropologists Reinvented Race, Sex, and Gender in the Twentieth Century* (New York: Doubleday, 2019).

To learn more about how organizational culture was first widely discussed in the business world, see Terrence Deal and Allan Kennedy's best selling book, *Corporate Cultures: The Rites and Rituals of Corporate Life* (Cambridge, Mass.: Perseus Books, 1982).

A first, and well-done, example of the study of Japanese companies and the concept of culture is *The Art of Japanese Management* by Richard Pascale and Anthony Athos (New York: Simon and Schuster, 1981).

The culture and performance research references in this chapter is described in detail in John Kotter and James Heskett's book, *Corporate Culture and Performance* (New York: Free Press, 1992).

The Business Roundtable's Statement on the Purpose of the Corporation can be found in full at https://opportunity .businessroundtable.org/ourcommitment/.

Chapter 7: Mergers and Acquisitions That Create Real Value

Finding well-researched estimates for the success of mergers and acquisitions is more difficult than we expected. There is a wide range of estimates of the failure rates, from 50 to 90%. Readers who are so inclined can review Anup Agrawal and Jeffrey Jaffe, "The Post-Merger Performance Puzzle," *Advances in Mergers and Acquisitions* (2000) 1: 119–156, and Clayton Christensen et al., "The Big Idea: The New M&A Playbook," *Harvard Business*

Review, March 2011. For a complete summary of the various estimates, see Godfred Koi-Akrofi, "Mergers and Acquisitions Failure Rates and Perspectives on Why They Fail," *International Journal of Innovation and Applied Studies* (July 2016) 17: 150–158.

In this chapter we mentioned the Daimler-Chrysler merger as an example of integration severely hampered by cultural differences. For more on how this "merger of equals" played out, see Bill Vlasic and Bradly Stertz's *Taken for a Ride: How Daimler-Benz Drove off with Chrysler* (New York: Harper Collins, 2000).

Chapter 8: Agile Methodologies That Build Sustained and Scalable Agility

For more on the unlikely story behind the development of the Agile Manifesto, see Caroline Nimbs Nyce, "The Winter Getaway that Turned the Software World Upside Down," *Atlantic*, December 8, 2017.

For the original Agile Manifesto, the principles, and the authors, visit http://agilemanifesto.org/.

For a look at the dual operating system in action, see John Kotter and Holger Rathgeber's fable, *That's Not How We Do It Here!* (New York: Portfolio/Penguin, 2016).

Chapter 9: Broad Social Initiatives That Can Help Billions

For more about the kind of tactics used by the Otpor movement and other social movements, see Srdja Popovic's *Blueprint for Revolution* (New York: Spiegel & Grau, 2015).

For a case study on the effectiveness of the Montreal Protocol, see Frederike Albrecht and Charles F. Parker, "Healing the Ozone Layer: The Montreal Protocol and the Lessons and Limits of a Global Governance Success

Story," in Mallory Compton and Paul Hart's *Great Policy Successes* (Oxford University Press, 2019) and Lisa Schaefer, *The Montreal Protocol,* Centre for Public Impact, September 3, 2019, https://www.centreforpublicimpact .org/case-study/the-montreal-protocol/.

Chapter 10: More Leadership from More People

There is no shortage of good books about Nelson Mandela and his leadership. For an absolutely wonderful book with insights into Mandela as a person and a leader, see his autobiography, *A Long Walk to Freedom* (Boston: Little, Brown and Company, 1994). For more about the story of how Mandela's seemingly simple actions during the 1995 Rugby World Cup were instrumental in changing the course of a nation, see John Carlin's *Playing the Enemy: Nelson Mandela and the Game That Made a Nation* (London: Penguin Press HC, 2008).

For more on Watson and IBM, see Kevin Money's *The Maverick and His Machines* (Hoboken, N.J.: John Wiley & Sons, 2003).

To see Dr. John Kotter's first in-depth writing on the differentiation between leadership and management, see his book *A Force for Change: How Leadership Differs from Management* (New York: Free Press, 1990).

To learn more about the idea of starting where the energy is, rather than focusing on getting resisters onboard, see Everett M. Rogers's *Diffusion of Innovations,* 5th ed. (New York: Free Press, 2003).

For more on creating psychological safety and encouraging productive failures, see Amy Edmondson, *Teaming: How Organizations Learn, Innovate, and Compete in the Knowledge Economy* (Hoboken, N.J.: John Wiley & Sons, 2012).

General References from Psychology and Neuroscience

Many researchers have written extensively about various approaches to mitigating Survive (largely in the field of anxiety research) and activating Thrive. Following is a selected list of some of those we have found most useful in our work.

Barbara L. Fredrickson is perhaps the most well-known researcher in the field of positive psychology. To learn more about her broaden-and-build theory, which highlights the impact of positive and negative emotions and the power of positive emotions, see B. L. Fredrickson, "The role of positive emotions in positive psychology: The broaden-and-build theory of positive emotions," *American Psychologist* (no. 3, 2001) 56: 218–226, https://doi.org/10.1037/0003-066X.56.3.218.

More and more companies are embracing mindfulness as a critical skill for employees. Ellen Langer has written extensively about mindfulness and its value in business. To learn more, see an interview with Ellen Langer at https://www.strategy-business.com/article/00310?gko=ddca6.

For more on the intersection of neuroscience and helping employees feel connected to and passionate about their work, see Daniel M. Cable's book, *Alive at Work: The Neuroscience of Helping Your People Love What They Do* (Boston: Harvard Business Review Press, 2018).

Martin Seligman is known as the founder of positive psychology. His extensive research spans decades and has influenced psychologists around the world. You can find numerous articles, books, and videos of his work on happiness and well-being. For more on his working on authentic happiness see his book *Authentic Happiness: Using the New Positive Psychology to Realize Your Potential for Lasting Fulfillment*, 6th ed. (New York: Free Press,

2002). For an in-depth look at his PERMA model of well-being (positive emotion, engagement, relationships, meaning, and achievement) see his book *Flourish: A Visionary New Understanding of Happiness and Well-Being* (New York and Toronto: Free Press, 2012).

For more on potential strategies to calm Survive, see Susan David and Christina Congleton's November 2013 *Harvard Business Review* article "Emotional Agility: How Effective Leaders Manage Their Negative Thoughts and Feelings."

Mihalyi Csikszentmihalyi is the founder of Flow theory and is known for his decades of work in the field of positive psychology. For more on his work on creativity (a key outcome of an activated Thrive channel), see his book *Creativity: Flow and the Psychology of Discovery and Invention* (New York: HarperCollins Publishers, 1996).

Acknowledgments

This book is the product of a formal research project that began four years ago. Our colleague at Kotter International, Russell Raath, had become intrigued by material he had been reading in what is broadly called "brain science." He had discovered that some findings from this broad domain helped explain in a new and better way why the intellectual property and consulting techniques he used worked well. Other findings raised interesting possibilities about what might work even better.

A study group was formed in our Cambridge office. In a series of two- to three-hour meetings, one every four to six weeks, we began to dig into the brain research, guided by questions like these:

- What does this work tell us about human nature that might be especially important for people living in today's era of increasingly rapid and complex change?

- More specifically, what does it tell us about why some individuals and organizations struggle so much to change when it is obviously needed?

- What does it tell us, if anything, about those few individuals and enterprises that handle change especially well?

- What is the simplest, most powerful way to think about human nature as it relates to the sort of questions listed above?

We also began talking to people who had been working in the brain science arena: medical doctors, psychologists, MD/PHD brain researchers.

From this effort came the Survive/Thrive model presented in this book.

In parallel, during this time, we and other colleagues at Kotter International launched and completed any number of smaller projects on what we have been learning from interactions with clients and potential clients around change challenges and the most common ways they presented themselves, associated with executing new strategies, restructuring, cultural renewal, mergers and acquisitions, and so on. And we read and talked to experts in order to put what we were finding in the broadest possible historical framework.

Among the people who have contributed greatly to all this work we owe a special thanks to Rachel Rosenfeldt, Nancy Dearman, David Carder, Rick Western, Kathy Gersch, Justin Wasserman, Maurizio Agresta, Tim Barefield, Pat Cormier, Danny Dworkin, Eric Ellis, Tanya Kruger, Maria Leister, Jimmy Leppert, Andres Mejia, Kristin Oberdorf, Kevin Waits, Martha Kesler, Nick Petschek, Holger Rathgeber, Celine Schillinger, Abby Ezra, Evan Smith, Tien Tran, Meredith Valdez, Rod Walker, and Cameron Welter—and all our other colleagues at Kotter International in our Seattle office, Cambridge office, and elsewhere (Los Angeles, New York, Atlanta, France, Germany, etc.). Also, thanks to our team at Wiley. Finally thanks to two non-Kotter people who helped our early discussions of brain science: Professor Richard Boyatzis at Case Western University in Cleveland, and Dr. Scott Rauch, the head of McLean Hospital in Boston.

To all—an astonishing group who know much about the difficult task of pioneering useable knowledge and helping others prosper with it—we owe our deepest thanks.

About the Authors

Dr. John P Kotter is the Konosuke Matsushita Professor of Leadership, Emeritus, at the Harvard Business School, a *New York Times* bestselling author, and a well-known thought leader in the areas of complex change, leadership, and corporate culture. He is also the co-founder of the management consulting firm Kotter International.

Dr. Kotter has published 21 books, 12 of which have been bestsellers and 13 of which have been honored on lists of best business or management books of the year. His recent book, *Accelerate*, is based on research done at Kotter International. The St. Petersburg Economic Forum, *Inc.* magazine, strategy+business, and the Chartered Management Institute all selected Accelerate as a best-of-year book. *Leading Change*, perhaps his most well-known book, has been translated into 26 languages and was chosen by *Time* magazine as one of the 25 most influential management books ever written.

A 2001 survey of 504 businesses by Bloomberg Businessweek reported that Dr. Kotter was seen as the number one leadership guru in America. Subsequent surveys by a number of organizations in 2004, 2008, 2009, and 2013–19 have named Dr. Kotter as the world's number one thought leader in the areas of management, corporate culture, and change. The Chinese edition of *Harvard Business Review* rated him as one of the six thought leaders who have "significantly influenced Chinese modern business ideas and practices."

In 2018, London-based Thinkers50 inducted him into its Management Thinkers Hall of Fame (a small number of people from around the world who are "the giants upon whose shoulders managers and leaders stand").

Three videos co-produced by Dr. Kotter have won national or international awards. Three stage plays based on his book *Our Iceberg Is Melting* (the first sponsored by the *Times* of India) have been produced and shown to audiences in Europe and Asia.

In 2009, Dr. Kotter co-founded Kotter International. The firm focuses on helping organizations and leaders deal more effectively with complex change of any sort: strategic, digital, cultural, M&A driven, restructuring, and more. Today it has corporate offices in Seattle and Boston, with outposts in Los Angeles, Delhi, Denver, Chicago, Nashville, D.C., Atlanta, New York, Miami, Paris, and Frankfort. Its goal is to be the leading firm of its kind in the world.

Kotter International helps clients accelerate change to solve problems and grab opportunities. Working side by side, Kotter empowers teams to inspire a movement, grounded in shared purpose, to create a lasting impact. Kotter clients regularly win awards for their joint work. In 2017 Kotter International itself won its first formal award: *Entrepreneur* magazine's "Top Company Cultures," in the small business category, ranking in first place among management consulting firms.

Dr. Kotter personally is the recipient of six lifetime achievement awards. The latest, from 2018, was given by the Best Practices Institute with the inscription "Kotter is a legend in the field of change."

Dr. Vanessa Akhtar has a background in Counseling Psychology, specializing in Sport and Performance Psychology. Before transitioning into the consulting world, she taught at Boston University and worked with teams, coaches, and athletes – ranging from youth through professional and Olympic-level – to help individuals reach the top of their game. She has published extensively in a variety of academic journals, presented at conferences around the United States, and co-authored a chapter in *Mindfulness and Performance* (Cambridge University Press).

Dr. Akhtar has worked with organizations around the globe, spanning a variety of industries – including healthcare, education, oil and energy, pharmaceuticals, nonprofits, advertising, and philanthropic foundations. Her ultimate goal is to help individuals and groups develop critical leadership skills, across all levels of organizations, to better meet the changing needs of today's complex environment. At Kotter, Vanessa works on the firm's most complex engagements, walking alongside clients throughout their transformation journey, in addition to helping driving Kotter's ongoing research and development efforts. She has written on the topics of leadership and change for outlets such as *Forbes*, Huffington Post, Chief Executive, Education News and *Training* magazine, and has provided commentary to a number of media outlets on the topics of employee engagement, supply chain transformation, and digital transformation.

Gaurav Gupta has worked across 3 continents and 10 countries and he attributes his perspective to this extensive global experience. Gaurav works with organizations and individuals to unleash potential and maximize business outcomes. His expertise is in change leadership and strategy execution. By combining thinking from behavioral science, leadership development, and strategy implementation, he has successfully advised leaders across industries as diverse as finance, food and beverage, oil and energy, healthcare, and chemicals on their most important business initiatives.

At Kotter, Gaurav researches and develops the most successful approaches to large-scale change implementation. Further, as the Kotter representative for the Asia-Pacific region, he shares insights gained from the application of leadership and change research through speaking engagements, consulting, and facilitated learning events.

Gaurav is also the co-founder of Ka Partners, a firm established to help growing startups perform better through greater employee engagement, more efficient resource utilization, and better decision-making.

Gaurav has spoken at conferences and delivered guest lectures. He has also published numerous articles in magazines like *Harvard Business Review* and *Forbes*, and has been quoted in publications like the *Wall Street Journal*, *Financial Times*, and *Crain's Chicago*. Gaurav combines his professional expertise with his interest in international development to serve as an executive board member for Medic to Medic, a nonprofit that sponsors medical students in Uganda and Malawi.